PRAISE FOR NO NONSENSE REAL ESTATE

As a 27 year professional real estate investor I can assure you that just one simple error can cost tens of thousands of dollars in the blink of an eye. Buying or selling a home is most likely the largest financial transaction that will ever take place for most people. You MUST be VERY well informed on all aspects of the deal.

Alex Goldstein is a PRO'S PRO. He not only knows what to say, but how to do it. Noting takes the place of experience and Alex has been there and done that. Read and learn.

-Jim Toner, Real Estate Investor for 3 Decades & Author of "The Consumer's Guide to Investment Real Estate"

Alex has put together an essential book that shows the reader he truly understands what the real estate buyer or seller really wants to know. He does so in a well-organized, thorough and easy to follow book I would recommend to anyone who values their own time and money.

-Matt Niño, Executive Vice President, Palm Harbor Homes

I invest a lot into real estate, so I know what the real deal is and what isn't. This is a very thorough review of what the intelligent homebuyer needs to know... straight from an experienced pro that has seen millions of dollars exchange hands at the closing table.

-Peter Voogd, #1 International Bestselling Author of 6 Months to 6 Figures

This book is filled with relevant and practical information that is easy to consume and digest. Every few pages I realized how important it is to pay attention to that particular detail to ensure a successful transaction. The fact that this is all coming from one of the premier thought leaders in the real estate industry makes me stand up and take notice.

-Jim Krautkremer, Owner of 2 Real Estate Brokerages, Investor, and Founder of Motivated Seller Blueprint

NO NONSENSE REAL ESTATE

ESSENTIALS EVERY CONSUMER SHOULD KNOW
BEFORE BUYING OR SELLING A HOME

BY
ALEX GOLDSTEIN

No Nonsense Real Estate: Essentials Every Consumer Should Know Before Buying or Selling a Home

© 2016 Alex Goldstein

Published by Influential Press

This publication is sold with the understanding that neither the author nor the publisher is engaged in rendering legal, accounting, financial or other professional service. If legal advice or other expert assistance is required, the services of a competent professional person should be sought.

DEDICATION

To my clients, who have entrusted me with life-changing decisions.

To my family, for whom no words can fully express my admiration and gratitude.

To my friends, who have helped and inspired me through booming markets and perilous busts.

To my beloved Tess, who graciously puts up with this crazy author.

TABLE OF CONTENTS

CHAPTER 1

DOES THE WORLD REALLY NEED ANOTHER REAL ESTATE BOOK?

He that is good for making excuses is seldom good for anything else.

— Benjamin Franklin

Why write a book on real estate when countless books already exist on the subject? Most real estate books are either so brief they aren't useful, or so dense they confuse more than clarify. This book aims to be in the middle. It provides enough information to be useful and practical, but not so much as to overwhelm the reader.

Buying or selling a home is one of the most significant financial decisions many people will ever make. Yet, too few people educate themselves before buying a home. Instead they rely entirely upon their agent and the other professionals they hire; but without a sound hiring process, how do they know they've got reliable advisors? There's a big difference between delegation and abdication, and after reading this book you will be better prepared to delegate without getting in over your head.

This book does not replace the services of professionals. You'll get the benefit of my experience over hundreds of millions of dollars of real estate transactions. You'll know what questions to ask and how the process works. Most importantly, the information in the following chapters will help you avoid unpleasant surprises. Nevertheless, you'll most likely be best served by hiring a team of professionals to work with you.

This book aspires to remain a valuable resource for many years by sticking to timeless essentials. I won't go deep into specifics that are likely to change from year to year. For this kind of information, please visit **Bonus.NoNonsenseBook.Com.** Kept online, that information will be updated as the world changes.

The big secret that the real estate industry won't tell you

Confession #1: Real estate agents are completely unnecessary.
Confession #2: The author of this book is a real estate agent.

It may seem crazy for a real estate agent to say that the whole profession isn't necessary. But this book promised no nonsense, and I don't get a special exemption. The fact of the matter is that a real estate agent should *only* be involved in a transaction when he/she can add value to that transaction. If the agent can't add value, then he or she has no legitimate reason to be involved.

There are two categories of value a real estate agent can add to a transaction:

1.   *Skill* – Specialized experience in a given market, or type of property. Uncovering hidden opportunities and investigating risks that would be missed by laypeople.

2.   *Service* – Reducing the time, effort, and stress the client expends on the transaction. Creating opportunities and financial gain that clients are unable or unlikely to get for themselves.

It's really that simple. If an agent doesn't offer skills relevant to your needs, or doesn't provide a level of service that makes your life better, then you may as well be going through the entire process alone.

A real estate agent is like a chef. A restaurant is only successful if it makes and serves incredible food. If a restaurant delivers all of these things, then people go to the restaurant. But nobody ever *needs* to go to a restaurant. You can go to a grocery store and cook at home.

The entire restaurant industry exists because it provides something that is either better, or more convenient, than what people can do at home. If that weren't the case, the whole industry would cease to exist. It's exactly the same in real estate. But most real estate agents don't acknowledge the simple fact that they're unnecessary. People can do this for themselves if they want to do so.

Of course, if the average person handles real estate transactions alone, he or she is probably going to make mistakes due to lack of experience. Those mistakes can be costly, and have consequences that are felt for a decade or more. And even if people do everything perfectly by themselves, they will have to spend a lot of time managing the process. Hence, there are plenty of valid reasons to use the services of a real estate agent.

Nevertheless, clients always have the choice to 'walk out of the restaurant and cook at home'—it's best to acknowledge this fundamental truth rather than dance around the issue. There's a big difference between a necessity and a convenience. Clients should demand a level of expertise and service that adds value. It may seem obvious that clients would want expert advisors who add value, and yet many people settle for far less.

In this book, we'll cover how to find the agents that deliver value. You'll also be better prepared to do things on your own, if you choose not to hire an agent.

Why listen to me?

This book represents experience gained from hundreds of millions of dollars in real estate negotiations. Not just as an agent representing people on their transactions, but as a principal in deals worth more than $50 million. I have hired many agents, and know what it's like to be the client. I have written the big checks, not just cashed them. This gives me unique empathy for what it's like on both sides of the table, both as client and agent.

For most people, real estate represents the largest financial decisions of their lives. Those decisions shouldn't be made in a vacuum, ignoring the larger financial picture. Yet most real estate agents have no experience with financial planning, stocks, bonds, or insurance. Earlier in my career, I was a bond trader and portfolio manager, with total discretion over $500 million. I've passed the Series 7 securities exam, as well as the life insurance licensing exam. This experience helps put real estate in the context of other financial decisions. We will do that together in this book, looking not just at real estate in isolation, but in relation to larger financial and personal decisions. The resources at **Bonus.NoNonsenseBook.Com** will also help you understand real estate's role in your overall financial plan.

It's my hope that my unique background and experience will help you get the best possible results, as quickly and easily as possible. Let's get started!

Before You Read Any Further, Get Your Free Bonus Materials

To help make the lessons in this book as actionable and easy-to-understand as possible, I've produced a free bonus video training for you.

Please visit **Bonus.NoNonsenseBook.com** for instant access.

In this video training exclusively for readers, we explore the key concepts of the book, dive deeper into them, and answer the most common questions I receive.

If you're making a real estate decision with loved ones, it's especially helpful to watch the videos together – before you make a deal, or even start looking at homes.

CHAPTER 2

HOUSING ECONOMICS SIMPLIFIED

The function of economic forecasting is to make astrology look respectable.

—J.K. Galbraith

Economics 101 tells us that supply and demand drive markets. But what does that mean, for homebuyers and sellers? How do you know when is a good time to buy or sell? How do you know whether you should negotiate or take the deal on the table? How do you know if you should compromise or walk away? In this chapter, we'll explore the numbers in the simplest terms and show you how to use them.

Two things drive every local real estate market. First is supply: the quality and cost of properties in the area. Second is demand: the number of buyers ready and able to buy. Once you understand how to use the data, you can make more effective decisions when buying or selling real estate.

Demand is driven by income, credit, and household formation. The more people earn, and the cheaper it is to borrow, the more they will spend on housing. But if borrowing costs rise, or if incomes shrink, people cannot spend as much on their next home. Household formation is driven by birth rates and immigration, offset by deaths and emigration.

Incomes at the local level can vary quite dramatically from the national averages. For example, when Wall Street is booming and bankers are getting big bonuses, New York City real estate prices can spike. But if oil prices fall, places dominated by oil-related jobs such as Texas can experience a decline in real estate prices. Significant changes at the local level are commonplace, even though they are not always obvious in the national income statistics.

On the other hand, credit conditions tend to be similar across the country. You won't find dramatically different trends in home mortgage rates in New York versus California, for example.

Credit conditions have less influence on some types of properties than others. The prices for high-end properties are less sensitive to swings in interest rates because buyers often pay in cash. On the other end of the real estate market, investors also often pay for low-end or distressed homes in cash. Thus, interest rates have less of an impact on properties priced at high and low extremes than on those in the middle, where buyers often use a mortgage to pay for a home.

For most homebuyers and sellers—those buying or selling average-priced homes—credit conditions are critical. Rising interest rates mean higher mortgage payments, making homes less affordable. Lower rates mean lower payments and more affordable homes. Thus, for mom and pop homes, credit conditions will have the greatest impact on demand.

Supply changes much more slowly than demand. Planning and developing homes often takes years. Some developments take a decade or more to go from concept to completion. So always remember that while demand can skyrocket quickly or drop precipitously at a moment's notice, supply moves more slowly.

When builders are ready to pour billions into development, they can't snap their fingers and dramatically increase supply. In some areas, zoning and environmental concerns add great uncertainty to the building process. Even when building is going up at a furious pace, it will never match the speed at which demand can rocket upward or crash down.

Think of the classic children's fable of *The Tortoise and the Hare:* supply is the tortoise, and demand is the hare. Supply chugs along and is always increasing, sometimes very slowly and sometimes quickly, but always increasing. Demand, however, can skyrocket or crash; it's volatile and fickle.

A primer on the numbers

There is an overwhelming flood of housing market statistics, published by countless government agencies and private entities. To avoid drowning in data, what follows is a guide to the most practical statistics. Importantly, we'll address some of the common ways people misuse and misunderstand these statistics.

Average sale price

The average sale price is deceptively simple, and often abused. What exactly is it an average of? Even small towns can have substantial differences in the average selling price between neighborhoods. For example, houses north of Main Street may be 8% more expensive than those south of Main Street. Trends are also important. Are the values for the homes south of Main Street catching up to the value of the homes north of Main Street?

Proper context is critical for making sense of the numbers. Whenever you see an average, make sure you know how the data set was defined. This simple oversight frequently leads people to make wildly inaccurate estimates of value. If you're starting the process by selecting a range of properties that's too broad or too narrow, the resulting valuation will be inaccurate.

Price per square foot (PSF)

The price per square foot provides an apples-to-apples comparison of different-size homes. The market price for a 3,000-square-foot home that costs $750,000 is $250 per square foot. All things being equal, a 4,000-square-foot house should cost $1 million by the same standards. But all things are not equal. The quality of interior finishes, size of the lot, and many other factors impact a home's value. PSF is a blunt instrument, useful but not precise.

Ask your agent to investigate if a home has a significantly different PSF than neighboring homes. Sometimes a seller is being unrealistic in the price they are asking. There can be subtle differences between neighboring homes that affect price.

Days on market (DOM)

The Days on Market number tells you how long the property has been for sale. If a home has been on the market for six months and most homes sell in two months, there may be a problem with the property. Or it may be overpriced. Or both. DOM can also tell you what's happening in the market. When there's a buying frenzy, you may see most homes go under contract their first day on the market. In a slump, the average may be many months.

Note that you may only see how long the current listing has been in place. This is not the same as the days it has been on the market. For example, if a home has been listed for six months and doesn't sell, they may start a new listing. If the Multiple Listing Service shows you the length of the current listing, you wouldn't know that the home has been languishing on market for a long time. Ask your agent to give you some insight into the history of the property, and any previous listings that may not be visible to you.

Months inventory

The number of months worth of inventory is the most important statistic to assess whether you're in a buyers' market, a seller's market, or a balanced market. It is based on the current absorption rate of the market and tells you how many months it would take for all homes to sell. The calculation is simple:

$$\textit{Months inventory} = \frac{\textit{Number of homes for sale}}{\textit{Number of homes sold in the prior month}}$$

If there were two months of inventory, every home on the market would sell within two months if no more became available. This low inventory indicates a seller's market and, likely, rising prices. But if the current market has 12 months of inventory, it's a buyers' market and prices are likely to soften.

The months inventory statistic can vary between neighborhoods and price points. For example, there may be six months of inventory in a metro area. But a high demand for homes priced between \$100,000 and \$200,000 could mean that there's only two months of inventory at that price point. It's important to look at the inventory by both geography and price point, to get a realistic sense of the market dynamics.

Age of construction

The age of the homes selling in the area can provide additional context for the other statistics. If prices stay the same but the average age of homes sold increases, people pay the same money for older houses. For example, the average price remains $500,000 in a neighborhood, but the homes sold are much older in year two, then people are getting less for their money. This is a price increase by stealth. Conversely if people are getting newer homes for the same price as they were paying for older homes a year before, then buyers are now getting more for their money. If you look at average prices, and ignore the age of construction, you'll miss a potentially significant trend.

Is it a good time to buy or sell?

Fundamentally, there are three types of real estate markets: a buyers' market, a seller's market, and a balanced market. It's easy to lose sight of this and drown in statistics, but just keep in mind that all the numbers boil down to just three types of markets. Below is a simple way to assess the current state of the market and make the numbers work for you.

Signs of a buyer's market:

- The average home takes more than six months to sell.
- Sellers will respond to virtually any offer, even unrealistic low-ball offers.
- Homes often sell at large discounts from asking prices.

Signs of a seller's market

- Homes sell in just days or weeks, and a home on market for a month is suspicious.
- Homes sell at or above the asking price.

- New records of price per square foot are repeatedly set.
- Desperate buyers write 'love letters' to sellers expressing appreciation for the home.

Signs of a balanced market

- Homes sell in two to four months.
- Selling prices are close to asking prices.
- Sellers aren't overconfident that a better buyer will come along, and buyers aren't certain they'll find a better home.

CHAPTER 3

PROS AND CONS OF WORKING WITH AGENTS

There are two reasons for everything — a good reason, and the real one.

— Winston Churchill

The polling organization Gannett reported that the American public views real estate agents in much the same way it views Congress: very negatively. A profession doesn't get a reputation *that* bad if it's wholly undeserved. Even your author—a real estate agent—understands and empathizes with distrusting real estate agents. I used the services of agents for over a decade before I became one myself, and the disappointing level of service is what motivated me to get my real estate license.

Nevertheless, there are numerous valid reasons for engaging an agent. First and foremost, managing a real estate transaction can be arduous. Transactions have many moving parts and high stakes. It's overwhelming when you don't know what you're doing. Even when you do know what you're doing, it can be a time-consuming and stressful endeavor. Secondly, the cost of making a mistake can be financially ruinous. Inviting the opinion of an experienced guide, or at least a second set of eyes, is a wise choice for one of the largest financial decisions of a lifetime. For these reasons and more, most people hire an agent to represent them.

Where things go wrong is when people engage an agent carelessly. Like hiring for any other job, the key is figuring out who is the best candidate before you hire him or her. Later, we'll cover in-depth strategies for finding an excellent agent. First, let's examine why there are so many agents out there who have disappointed so many clients.

Where the problems began

Why are there so many horror stories about real estate agents? Why do people perceive real estate agents' general level of service as much lower than that of lawyers or accountants? The most obvious culprit is the fact that barriers to entry are relatively low in the real estate profession. Requirements vary from state to state, but on the whole, it's not a major investment of time or money to become a licensed agent. People who don't know what to do with their careers jump into real estate simply because they can.

Most licensed agents come to the profession without experience and are learning on the job. Many of those who stay in the profession never develop the competency and connections to provide excellent service. Unfortunately, the majority of licensed agents only complete the legally mandated minimum training. Hundreds of thousands of licensed agents work part-time, and many don't even close a single transaction in a given year.

The public has a right to expect more, especially given how much money is at stake. Real estate professionals should give insightful, useful guidance. The requisite experience is acquired on the ground by doing lots of transactions. In the best-case scenario, agents have not only represented other people, but have the experience of conducting many transactions on their own behalf. Nothing makes a real estate agent more empathetic to the client than having worked with his or her own money on the line. Licensing may only demand basic competency, but clients have a right to demand true professionalism.

The client is not always right.

While we're being totally no nonsense about the real estate profession, it's only fair to divulge client contributions to the problem. In simplest terms, the client is not always right. This may be shocking to some. However, acknowledging this fact helps avoid common mistakes.

When are clients wrong? Clients are wrong when they don't demand expertise from agents. It would seem to be common sense that every person demands expertise and professionalism. Unfortunately, there are countless examples to the contrary.

The most common example of the client making the wrong move is when people give their business to a family member or a social acquaintance. They do so out of generosity, trying to help that person build their business. However, buying or selling a home is a significant decision. It affects your personal finances, as well as your family's lifestyle and well-being.

Here's a case study of how this decision can go wrong. A newsletter subscriber called to express how impressed she was with the weekly newsletter I write. She was convinced I was supremely qualified, committed, and a clear expert in the market. She couldn't have been more flattering.

I assured this woman that if we worked together, she would have the best home-buying experience possible. There was an awkward pause. Then she said, "Well, I'm dying to work with you, but I've been arguing with my husband. He insists upon hiring my know-nothing brother-in-law."

She continued, "We want to buy a bank foreclosure and my brother-in-law has never done this type of transaction before. He doesn't even work in this area. It's stupid. I could scream!"

This couple was making one of the most significant financial decisions of their lives, but they chose to hire someone they knew was unqualified. A lot of people make the same mistake. These common occurrences bring down industry standards. Clients who hire an agent based on a personal connection instead of competency keep unqualified agents in the business. Clients think they're "doing them a favor." In reality, this favor often brings financial distress to the client.

It can be hard to say "no" to friends and family. But the stakes in a real estate transaction are significant. Any problems that arise from the transaction may harm the relationship you were trying to preserve by saying "yes." Mixing business with personal relationships is *always* fraught with danger.

Award your business to the agent who shows high competency and drive. Failing to do so not only puts a great deal of money at risk, it may also damage the personal relationship you were trying to save. If you come to regret your decision, feeling as though you paid the wrong price or bought in the wrong neighborhood, the effects linger. It stings every time you see that family member or friend you were trying to help.

What great agents do that mediocre ones don't

The most important thing agents can do for their clients is to help them make sound decisions.

Their role is not simply to provide information, but to curate it. Agents must help clients understand what's meaningful from the huge amount of information available. This ability only comes with experience and commitment.

A great real estate agent should provide information and analysis without expectation of immediate compensation. The agent should radiate enthusiasm and expertise. They should go well above the minimum standards to be educated about the profession and about business in general. There's a lot at stake, and it makes no sense to work with someone who takes a half-baked approach.

In sum, they should be committed to the profession, and it should show. As the entertainment and fashion mogul Russell Simmons put it: "Imagine if a comedian said, 'Sorry, I can't be funny right now because nobody's paying me.' It's a comedian's job to be funny all of the time." A great real estate agent is someone who is enthusiastic about real estate and provides top-caliber service as a matter of reflex.

Six benefits of working with a real estate agent

1. MLS Access

Numerous websites such as Zillow have done a great service in providing real estate information to the public. However, none of them are as accurate as the data supplied to realtors: specifically, the local MLS (Multiple Listing Service). Relying on sources other than the MLS means relying on outdated and often erroneous information. We want to avoid the disappointment of falling in love with a home that's not available, or basing values on a comparable sale that's totally outdated. Thus, it's best to have a realtor set you up with curated MLS searches targeted to your needs.

2. *Valuation*

Appraisals are just estimates. They do not reflect what a property will sell for—only the actual sale price dictates true value. Here's where appraisers and agents differ: appraisers are paid to estimate; agents are paid to get deals done. If an agent is consistently unable to predict the sales price within a reasonable margin of error, they can't put food on the table. Appraisers don't have that type of urgency regarding their appraisals.

This isn't to say appraisals aren't valuable. Appraisals contain a lot of helpful information, and ultimately they underpin the whole system of real estate lending. However, any given appraisal can be inaccurate. Furthermore, appraisers are often asked to cover very wide areas. In these cases, their local knowledge isn't as current or deep as an agent who is expert in the area.

It is worth noting that appraisers ultimately work for bureaucrats at large banks, and under the oversight of the government. Appraisers are lot more concerned with keeping that business than anything else, and their incentives may not be the same as yours.

Automated valuation services like Zillow are also notoriously inaccurate—even the CEO of Zillow admits a median error rate of 8%. 8% is a significant variance, and the actual error rate may be much higher. For example, the LA Times reported numerous metro areas where Zillow's median error rate was staggering (12% in San Francisco and 20% in New York City). An experienced agent will be able to provide a valuation that accurately reflects the price at which a sale will actually close.

3. Negotiation

Negotiation is such a critical piece of a transaction that there's a whole chapter devoted to it in this book. You may negotiate deals all the time in the course of your work, but it's still helpful to have a real estate specialist run your negotiations on a home. There's emotion involved, and it can cloud your perspective in a way that doesn't happen at work.

Ideally, you will find someone who has closed millions of dollars in property sales in your area. Even better if they've negotiated millions of dollars in transactions as a principal. Please see the chapter on negotiations to learn more. For now, suffice it to say that even experienced negotiators may be well served by having a professional working on their behalf.

4. Off-market listings

Agents who network in the neighborhood will know about homes where the owner is willing to sell but hasn't listed the home. Similarly, they will know of buyers who want something so specific that they'll only take action when a perfect home comes to market. These sorts of off-market transactions can be great for both buyer and seller, and are very unlikely to happen without an experienced agent.

In 2014, 15% of homes sold in Denver were never listed on the MLS, according to the *Wall Street Journal*. In Silicon Valley 17% of sales were off MLS, and in Washington DC the figure was 8.5%. Wherever you live, it's safe to say that some important homes will be sold without going on MLS. This alone makes it worth working with an agent specializing in the area. Otherwise, you're virtually certain to miss significant opportunities.

5.   *Vetted referrals*

Every real estate transaction requires a variety of professionals. Rather than hoping for the best with an inspector, attorney, or lender, turn to an agent for introductions to professionals with proven track records. If you're relying on people who haven't been thoroughly vetted, it can make your transaction difficult, expensive, and even painful. An experienced agent's network is a *major* asset to buyers and sellers that's often overlooked.

6.   *What you don't know can hurt you.*

Without proper guidance, you may be limiting your options unnecessarily. For example, you may not know about financing options that are available to you, limiting yourself in your search as a result. Conversely, you may be considering options that are best left off the table. For example, there may be problems with a certain street or neighborhood that aren't obvious but could be very important. You may be contemplating a remodel in an area where that expense is unlikely to yield a return.

To reap the greatest benefit, it's important to provide your agent with as much information as possible. Tell your agent what you want in as much detail as possible. Also explain any limitations or constraints you think you have. If an agent is only working with half the picture, they can't deliver optimal results.

CHAPTER 4

SPECIAL CIRCUMSTANCES

To hell with circumstances; I create opportunities.

— Bruce Lee

Some circumstances require special consideration and advice. If any of the following apply to you, please read on:

- Buying a new home while you still own a home
- First-time home buyers
- Building a new home
- Divorcing couples
- A Non-U.S. citizen is the buyer or seller

Buying a new home while you still own one

Should you buy a new home before you sell the one you own? Nobody wants to pay for two houses when they only need one. Here are some considerations to help you make the decision:

1.   Is it a buyer's market or a seller's market?

Since selling your home in a strong buyer's market can take a long time, start by initiating the sale. In a seller's market, the opposite is true, and you'll want to secure the purchase first. To assess whether your market favors buyers or sellers, please review Chapter Two.

But what if it's a balanced market? The specifics of your situation will determine when it's best to start. How quickly does your agent think your home will sell? How much can you expect to get for it? After you've got a handle on these things, review your expectations for your new home with your agent. Buying may take longer than selling if you're looking for a type of home that's not readily available, or if your budget is unrealistic.

2.   How much equity is in your home?

The equity in your home is defined as the value of the home, after subtracting the amount of debt on the property. For example, if you own a home worth $500,000 and you have a $300,000 mortgage, then you've got $200,000 in equity.

If you have a substantial amount of equity in your home, you can afford to be incorrect about the fair market value and still sell the home. You have room to maneuver. Continuing the example above, if the best offer you receive is only $450,000, that's still well over the $300,000 debt on the property. You can still buy a home you love and move on, even if the sale of your old home is not as profitable as you'd wished.

On the other hand, if there's not much equity in your home, selling is the first priority. You just don't have much margin for error, so it makes sense to get the sale sorted before contemplating a purchase.

Putting a home under contract before locking down the sale can be stressful when there's not much wiggle room on the sale price.

3. Should you use contingencies to protect yourself?

You can write contingencies into your contract to protect yourself from paying for two homes at the same time. For example, you could write an offer to purchase a home contingent upon the sale of your existing home within 60 days. This protects you if something goes awry with the sale of your home.

However, by using such a contingency you are asking the person on the other side to share your risk. They will likely want to be compensated for the risk and you'll pay more. Contingencies are insurance. You pay a premium when you buy insurance. It may not show up as a line item on your contract, but it's there. A buyer *without* contingencies will usually get the best price.

Lean on your real estate agent to help sort through these considerations and craft the best opening offer.

First-time homebuyers

First-time buyers typically buy as soon as they can afford to do so. Consequently, at the start of the buying process a mortgage lender may play an even more important role than a real estate agent. There are many mortgage lenders out there beyond your bank. A great real estate agent will help find a mortgage lender with a history of delivering results. Don't get discouraged if you get turned down. There are many lenders, each with different underwriting standards. A lender may reject a person one week, and approve the same person the next week.

Your next step after considering mortgage options is to understand the tax consequences. The U.S. tax code favors homeowners over renters. You may have more money in your pocket at the end of the year, even if the mortgage payment is larger than your rent. Meet with an accountant to crunch the numbers. Your real estate agent can refer you to a vetted professional.

If you don't track your personal finances, start now. An accountant isn't going to be able to provide you with an accurate analysis if you hand over a shoebox of receipts. Carefully monitor your finances to maximize your tax benefits. There are many websites and software packages to help, and your accountant can help you get oriented. Buying your first house is a great incentive to get finances in order.

Another important consideration may be finding a reliable contractor before starting the purchase process. First-time buyers can rarely afford a home that meets all of their desires. Remodeling an older home is an attractive option, allowing buyers on a budget to get the neighborhood and amenities they want. There's a reason the oldest real estate proverb is "buy the worst house in the best location."

Turning the worst house into a cozy home can be a massive project. It will be much easier if you use a reliable and fair contractor. There's another proverb, "the only thing more expensive than hiring a professional is hiring an amateur." Don't hire the contractor with the lowest bid. Only hire a contractor referred by a trusted source after a *recent* job. For most people this source is their agent.

Given all of the above, it is especially important for first-time buyers to work with a knowledgeable, experienced real estate agent. Since you probably won't be buying a mansion, you may not attract the attention of the most prominent real estate agent in your area. But a smart agent knows that if she does a good job, she'll have a customer for life.

Building a new home

Everyone fantasizes about building a dream house. This home has every feature and amenity one could want. It's in the perfect location. There are no plumbing or electrical problems; everything works effortlessly.

Making this dream a reality is where it gets complicated. The mistakes associated with buying land and building a home can be among the costliest errors in real estate.

The first step is finding a lot upon which to build your home. As they say, "Location, location, location!" Location affects value, and you want to protect your investment.

Costs can vary dramatically between lots that may appear similar. Building costs are affected by factors like soil composition, access to utilities, and variations in zoning restrictions and homeowners' association rules. Bring your builder to look at the piece of land you are considering and *make sure the builder is experienced in that area.* There are zoning and planning pitfalls specific to different communities.

In many areas it is best to buy an existing home and tear it down. There will already be utility hook-ups, so you won't have to worry about the costs associated with empty lots that don't have sewers, water, gas, and electricity.

It's important to construct your home to retain its value, even if you plan on never moving. Your home may be a significant part of your estate, and you may want to borrow against it. In every city, there's always the quirky house that the owners built solely to please themselves. This house is hard to sell, and often becomes a great burden when circumstances change.

Don't leave out features that buyers expect. For example, a modest closet may suit your clothing collection. But what if the next owner expects a massive walk-in closet? Even if you don't need a large closet, it may be worth a relatively small additional investment to protect the value of your home.

Consult with your real estate agent while planning your home so that you don't forget any important features. Even if you plan never to sell, protect the value of your home. There's too much money at stake to ignore details that can have a large impact on market value.

Divorcing couples

A home is often a couple's largest single asset, and the marital home may be at the center of a divorce settlement. It is important to understand both the economic realities, and your legal rights before making any major decisions.

Valuation becomes especially important when one spouse will keep the property, and the other will receive money in the divorce settlement. Couples often choose to avoid valuation disputes by selling the home and letting the market set the price. Your real estate agent can give you a range of likely selling prices, but it's up to the divorcing parties to determine how to proceed. Children often influence the decision whether to sell, since it may be best for the children to avoid the additional turmoil of moving.

Further complicating matters, part of a home's value may not be a marital asset. This is often true when one spouse came into the marriage with the property. Rules about how property is divided in a divorce vary by state, so the division of assets may not be as simple as splitting the market value of the house.

Remember the previous section about not relying on personal connections when choosing an agent? It can be especially tempting to lean upon a personal connection during a divorce. But it can also be counterproductive. First and foremost, the other spouse may second-guess the motives of the real estate agent. Also, a difficult transaction may stress that personal relationship. It is doubly important to turn to a neutral, professional real estate agent during a divorce.

Non-U.S. citizen is buyer or seller

The Foreign Investment in Real Property Tax Act (a.k.a. FIRPTA) governs transactions involving non-U.S. citizens. It applies to all real estate sellers who are not U.S. citizens. If you are a U.S. citizen buying from a non-U.S. citizen, you need to be aware of the law. The burden for compliance lies on the *buyer*, so the IRS will pursue the buyer if the seller doesn't comply. Also, the closing may be delayed or derailed if the seller makes a mistake. The bottom line is make sure you hire an escrow officer who is very experienced with FIRPTA transactions.

FIRPTA requires compliance with tax rules and may require a withholding of 15% of the property's sale price. If sellers don't calculate their numbers with proper withholding, and they were counting on those funds to close, the transaction can get stuck in limbo. Hence, full disclosure and an understanding of FIRPTA are particularly essential when a non-U.S. citizen is selling the property.

Many escrow companies will not accept foreign checks. Non-U.S. citizen buyers should be prepared to wire all funds required for the escrow. Also, purchase of the property is a separate matter from a buyer's visa and immigration rights. Thus, foreign buyers should consult with an attorney on immigration issues before getting into a real estate transaction. If you plan to become a U.S. citizen, there may also be tax implications. Always consult your tax advisor in advance of signing a contract.

In short, transactions involving non-U.S. citizens are more complex than normal. You can avoid unpleasant surprises by talking to advisors in advance and regularly throughout the transaction. The rules, regulations, opportunities, and programs for non-U.S. citizens change frequently.

CHAPTER 5

CHOOSING THE BEST HOME FOR YOUR FAMILY

It is our choices that show what we truly are, far more than our abilities.

—*J. K. Rowling*

Know your "why"

In any endeavor, it's impossible to know if the goal has been reached if the goal isn't clearly defined. Many people start their home search simply by seeing what's out there. There's nothing wrong with that, but it's much more effective to define the ideal outcome clearly at the start. People often regret decisions made when the goal is ambiguous.

Prior to getting serious about finding a new home, ask yourself and your family serious questions about your motivation for moving. Outline the reasons you are unsatisfied with your current home. Note the things you find yourself saying: "I only wish we had _____ or we could do _____ at home." It's often the little things that mean the most to our day-to-day lives.

Prioritize these wants. You probably won't find the *perfect* home right within your budget. Compromises are inevitable. But without clarifying your priorities from the outset you'll end up chasing your tail. You could also lose a great opportunity while you're debating a decision due to lack of clarity. Here are some important questions to ask at the beginning:

Are you motivated by investment (value) or consumption (lifestyle)?

Some people live for the deal, and others will sacrifice a deal to enhance their lifestyle. Do you want the fairly priced home that has everything on your wish list? Or would you take the great deal that has a few things missing?

There is no right or wrong answer, but being unclear which side of the fence you're on makes the whole process more difficult. Furthermore, if two people are making the decision and each has a different perspective, it's better to resolve the difference early on. The dealmaker may veto the perfect house, or the lifestyle seeker could put the kibosh on the deal of a lifetime. Decide which agenda gets the tie-breaking vote *before* you start, to de-personalize the decision and avoid hurt feelings.

What amenities are essential?

Everyone has their must-haves and their pet peeves. Decide what your deal breakers are, and which features would just be nice to have. Some buyers absolutely refuse to live without a walk-in pantry. Others can't imagine living without a pool. Make a list of your deal breakers. Being honest and specific about what you want will save you time.

If there is more than one decision-maker, it will be important to determine the priorities at the outset. Often, one partner must compromise a bit more than the other. It helps to discuss potential compromises *before* looking for homes. When the emotions start to run high on a property someone has fallen in love with, it becomes very difficult to talk sensibly about compromise. However, if you can fall back to a previous decision made mutually, it's easier to move forward.

Do you want a new neighborhood more than a new home?

Sometimes your current home is just right, but the area is not. You may want a better school or shorter commute. Investigate the area thoroughly, so that you don't trade old problems for new problems. Look at the schools, crime, parks, and restaurants. Drive and walk through the neighborhood. Don't make the mistake of trading the devil you know for the devil you don't, as the saying goes.

Calculate your means

It's a delicate dance between what you can afford and what you may desire. It's easy to fall in love with a home that pushes the boundaries. Sometimes it's acceptable to invest more than anticipated, particularly when contemplating a long-term move. Did you find a home that you expect to be in for at least 10 years? If so, then stretching your budget may be a wise decision – why be stuck with something you don't really love for the long term? Alternatively, if major changes such as a new job or more children are likely, spending more than you planned is riskier. The market can fluctuate and you don't want to be stuck house poor at a time you'd prefer to sell.

It's also critical to remember that lending standards change constantly. If the lending environment is favorable, this may impact your thinking about how much to spend on your next home. If rates are likely to rise, stretching the budget now becomes more sensible; otherwise your next move will be doubly expensive, at a higher price and interest rate.

At any given time, there will probably be a lender willing to loan you an amount that is not financially prudent. The basic measurement of housing affordability is PITI (Principal, Interest, Taxes, and Insurance) divided by gross income:

$$\frac{Housing\ affordability}{ratio} = \frac{Principal + Interest + Taxes + Insurance}{Gross\ income}$$

Some financial gurus like Dave Ramsey tell people to buy their homes for cash. But that's impractical for most people. The next most conservative standard is the 25% Rule. Simply put, if your cost of housing is no more than 25% of your gross income, then you're being financially conservative. You can go as high as you wish, especially if you expect your income to grow, but you're unlikely to get into trouble with the 25% Rule.

Of course, housing is just one expense. You'll want to factor other financial obligations into your decision. The debt-to-income ratio takes into account obligations beyond PITI:

$$Debt - to - income\ ratio = \frac{PITI + Debt\ payments}{Gross\ income}$$

It's prudent to keep this ratio at or below 36%. If you don't have any debts, and don't plan to incur any, you may consider increasing your housing budget beyond what the 25% Rule (which doesn't take into account non-real estate related debt) would suggest. In other words, take the total financial picture into account when determining your budget. Just as it's unwise to be overextended, there's no sense denying yourself a better home if it wouldn't be irresponsible to do so.

Whatever you decide, get pre-approved for your loan before negotiating. Your offer won't have much credibility if you can't prove your ability to consummate the purchase. Choose a lender who has a recent history of closing deals, which isn't necessarily the same as the lender advertising the best rates. Your real estate agent can point you to lenders who live up to their promises, and have a history of smooth transactions.

Beware of the largest hidden cost

There's an old expression in real estate that if you can't afford to live near the center of the city, just keeping driving until you qualify. Prices often drop as you get further away from the city center, but are these homes really more affordable? The cost of commuting is higher than most people realize.

According to a study by the Urban Land Institute, once your daily commute exceeds a few miles, your total cost of housing and transportation increases. They estimate that each mile of driving costs an extra $100,000 over the average worker's life. If you commute 30 miles each day, that's $3 million! If you're deciding between two neighborhoods, transportation costs can help make the decision easy.

The damage of a long commute is even worse when gasoline prices are high. Not only does your daily commute cost more, but the value of the home declines as other homebuyers run away from the high cost. When gas prices are low, people are especially prone to underestimate the importance of this hidden cost. Pay attention to the long-term, and keep in mind that volatile oil prices can great influence the value of a home far from employment centers.

The most insidious cost of commuting is the toll it takes on people's personal lives. Nobody is happy about a long commute, but most people don't realize how damaging it really is. One widely cited academic study indicated that long commutes are linked to divorce. When one partner commutes more than 45 minutes, there's a 40% higher rate of divorce than when neither spouse commutes that length of time. A study by UCLA researchers showed that the strongest correlation with obesity, of every factor studied, was commuting distance. Other studies have linked commuting with back pain, stress, and fewer social connections. There are so many reasons to avoid a lengthy commute that one must seriously consider any apparent financial savings very carefully.

Assemble your team

Choosing a real estate agent is so important that this book has a whole chapter on it. A real estate agent will help you assemble the rest of the team you'll need. Here is a brief overview of the people likely to be involved in your real estate transaction:

Escrow officer

The escrow officer is the main conduit for every element of the transaction. She will coordinate documents, funds, and the transfer of title. An escrow officer can make a transaction easy... or a nightmare. Ideally, choose your escrow officer based on your agent's recent successful closings. If you cannot choose your escrow officer, establish a good relationship and consistent communication the first day escrow is opened.

Title insurance representative

Most people will deal only with the escrow officer, who will order title insurance supplied by their firm. However, in some cases, the escrow officer will not be involved in the title insurance process. In these circumstances, contact the title insurance representative as soon as the deal is signed to ensure there are no problems with the title.

Property insurance agent

Most homebuyers won't have any difficulty securing insurance coverage. In some cases, though, it may be impossible or prohibitively expensive. Confirm the cost of insurance during your inspection period, so that you can get out of the deal if necessary. A history of claims on the property or elsewhere in the neighborhood could lead to a big challenge getting insurance coverage.

Home inspector

Home inspection is critical, and the selection of inspector is too often left to chance. There are two criteria for the ideal inspector: thoroughness and clear communication. Some inspectors are more detail-oriented than others. Even among the most meticulous inspectors, however, the quality of inspection reports varies dramatically.

Your inspector should explain the significance of the findings in a professional report. It's not sufficient to receive a laundry list of problems. You'll want to know what's important, what's insignificant, and why. For the best chance of buyer and seller reaching agreement on repairs, deliver a report that's authoritative and organized. For all of these reasons, a trusted recommendation is especially important when selecting an inspector.

Lender

Some lenders will promise you the world. Then, right before closing, there's a flurry of last-minute questions and document requests that call the loan into question. Being left at the altar by a lender is one of the most common reasons a transaction goes awry. Make sure that the lender you choose has recently closed transactions that went smoothly. Your real estate agent will be able to direct you to lenders who get deals done.

Appraiser

The lender will usually order the appraisal without your input. If you have any concerns, make sure that the agents supply the appraiser with the relevant information. If there's a big difference between the home you're buying and the surrounding homes, for example, don't leave things to chance. Similarly, if you're buying in an area that hasn't had closings in a while, have your agent gather data to help the appraiser to understand what's happening in the area.

Attorney

In some states, an attorney is involved in all real estate transactions. In others, they're seldom involved. When an attorney is involved, do a thorough vetting. Many transactions have been derailed by an attorney who was out of his depth or slow to respond. Remember, one attorney is not necessarily as good as another when it comes to real estate; attorneys may solicit business for all manner of legal issues, and passing the bar is no guarantee that an attorney is an expert on real estate. Stick to an attorney who specializes in real estate, and get referrals to avoid problems.

Accountant

The tax implications of real estate are significant and constantly changing. Consult with your accountant early and often. Not all accountants are equally knowledgeable about real estate, and it may be worth consulting with a specialist in real estate taxation. The accountant's role is particularly important when buying an investment property.

Time for action

Upon completion of the previous steps, you will have an excellent foundation upon which to find your next home. Remember the proverb, "perfect is the enemy of good." You should have high standards and demand the very best that you can find for your money. But don't waste time chasing unreasonable expectations. Setting the bar unrealistically high results in frustration and disappointment.

Virtually everyone makes *some* compromises on their home purchase. Whether you forgo some amenities or exceed your budget, it's rare to find everything you want at the exact price you'd hoped. Prioritizing from the start enables you to feel confident that you're getting a quality home and only making compromises when reasonable and necessary. When priorities aren't absolutely clear from the start, compromise becomes more stressful.

Of course, you could get lucky and find an extraordinary home at a bargain price. It's a great feeling when it happens. But it's easy to mess up even this opportunity when left to our own devices. When a great deal comes along, some people get greedy, or doubt it because they think it must be too good to be true. Lean on the experts you've hired to keep you from making an error.

Regardless of your area, your needs, or your circumstances, take action. If you don't start writing offers, you won't know your options. The house that looks like its overpriced may become a deal once the negotiations start – but you'll never know unless you get the ball rolling. Motion beats meditation.

CHAPTER 6

CONDOMINIUMS, CO-OPS, AND SINGLE FAMILY HOMES

Charity begins at home, and justice begins next door.

— *Charles Dickens*

This book generally refers to "homes" and "houses" as shorthand for single-family residences. Many of the same considerations apply to condominiums and co-ops, but not all of them. This chapter examines the differences between single-family homes and condominiums. Each type of property has different rights, responsibilities, and expenses.

Single-family homes

Single-family homeowners generally own the structure and the surrounding land. The homeowner is responsible for all utilities, taxes, insurance, and maintenance. Single-family homes often cost more than similar condos or co-ops, and offer the most privacy and flexibility.

Single-family homeowners can use their property as they wish as long as they follow local regulations. Most localities permit homeowners to paint a home any color, landscape, build a shed, or store an RV. However, if the home is in a community with a homeowners' association (HOA), there will be additional restrictions. Investigating the rules, restrictions, and finances of the HOA is as important as investigating the home itself.

Condominiums

The owner of a condominium typically owns the interior walls, floors, and appliances of her specific unit. All owners in the building jointly own building and common areas. Common areas include lobbies, gyms, swimming pools, parking areas, and other shared facilities. Each owner can use the common areas. But there may be rules and restrictions on use.

The owner must maintain and repair the interior of his unit. The condominium association maintains the exterior and common areas. The association also often pays the costs of sewer, water, and trash removal. The owner pays for utilities related to his unit.

It generally costs less to build a condo than a single family home, due to economies of scale. Condos can also be more energy-efficient. It's important to be aware that homeowners' associations can make special assessments. If the association is mismanaged, or an unexpected expense arises, the association can demand that all the owners cover a shortfall. Provided there are no unexpected shortfalls, a condo is often less expensive than a single-family house of comparable size.

Co-ops

Co-ops (an abbreviation for "housing cooperatives") are uncommon, except New York City, and some parts of the Midwest and Florida. Co-ops are like condos in that they're apartments in a building with shared common areas. However, they have a different ownership structure, which has many implications for owners.

A co-op owner doesn't own her home. Instead, she has shares in a corporation that owns the building. She leases the unit for as long as she holds her shares. The practical implications of co-ops are that they can be more difficult to buy for the following reasons:

- **Vetting by the co-op board** – You may have to audition before the co-op board and convince them you're a good fit. The level of vetting can be intense. Buildings in New York are famous for rejecting even wealthy celebrities.

- **High interest rates** – When buying a condo, the lender acquires collateral on which they can foreclose in the event of default. For a co-op the lender only has the shares as recourse. Co-op buyers thus face higher interest rates since it may be a greater risk for the lender.

- **Higher down payment** – The co-op board may require a higher down payment than the lender. This is to assure the financial stability of the corporation. While good for the co-op, more of your money is tied up in the property.

- **Tax complications** – Claiming a tax deduction on a co-op is more complicated than for a condo or single family home. Review the matter with a tax professional before purchasing so you know your after-tax cost.

Why would anyone buy a co-op? The quality of the building may make it worth jumping through hoops. Some people appreciate that the co-op board thoroughly vets all owners, and consider this a benefit.

Homeownership limitations

While single-family homes offer more flexibility and fewer restrictions than condos and co-ops, there are limitations to such homes. All homes are subject to city, county, and state regulations and taxation. In some towns, local regulations are quite permissive, and others may be more restrictive.

Planned subdivisions usually have their own set of rules and regulations. In some communities, homeowners can use their property however they like. But in others it can feel like the homeowners' association is trying to make life difficult. Before buying a home, examine the regulations, which may include:

- Maximum square footage or rules against additions
- Prohibition on storage buildings or added structures
- Yard and landscape requirements
- Prohibition of boat or RV storage
- Rules for exterior appearance such as paint colors, siding, or roof materials
- Restriction on animals, including some dog breeds
- Limits on the number of vehicles that can be permanently parked at the home
- Limits on antenna type and size
- Limits on the number of residents
- Age restrictions for senior communities

These are just some examples of common restrictions; there are countless others. Associations can levy fines for violating the rules.

They can also place liens for non-payment of dues and fines. Take these matters seriously and investigate before consummating a purchase.

Lifestyle factors favoring condos and co-ops

Renting an apartment is a viable alternative to owning a single-family home, but has serious limitations:

- Rents may rise
- You can't modify a rental the same way you can your own property
- You don't build equity
- A condominium or co-op can be the ideal alternative to renting. It protects against rising rents, allows customization, and has the potential to appreciate in value.

For many buyers, the decision comes down to age and lifestyle. Second-home owners and retirees may not want the hassle of caring for a single family home. Condos may be the only option for buyers in big cities who want a short commute.

For some, condos and co-ops have an advantage over single-family homes from a social perspective. The common areas in a condo or co-op building can be a place to spark new friendships, or forge business relationships.

Cost savings in a condo/co-op

The cost of a condo or co-op per square foot is generally less than that of a house. Thus, the mortgage will be less expensive. In some markets, though, condos are concentrated in prime locations and may offer no savings over single-family homes.

Monthly dues and special assessments can make condos and co-ops look expensive. But it's important to compare apples-to-apples. For a condo or a co-op, there is a monthly maintenance fee that covers the things you'd pay separately as the owner of a single-family house. For example, water, sewers, and trash are often part of that monthly payment. Also, the repair and maintenance of major building components such as exterior paint, roof, and insurance on the building structure are all covered in these monthly fees.

Neighborhoods that are dominated by houses are unlikely to also have a large concentration of condos/co-ops and vice versa. Thus, comparing single-family homes and condos may be like comparing apples to oranges, since their locations aren't truly comparable. Look at other factors such as commuting distance, schools, and neighborhood amenities. They impact your finances even though they aren't on the closing statement.

Special considerations for condos and co-ops

Poor management and inattentive owners can create a fiscal nightmare. An association must have adequate reserves for renovations and unexpected repairs. Raising condo fees in reaction to careless management burdens owners. It also makes resale difficult. Owners then have to pay up or sell at unfavorable prices. A condo or a co-op buyer should investigate the quality of the physical building, and its management, to avoid unpleasant surprises.

Lenders and government agencies that guarantee mortgages set special rules for condo appraisals. They include an examination of the finances and reserves. Lenders may refuse to grant a mortgage if a single party owns too many units in a project, or if too many are vacant or in foreclosure.

When condominiums don't meet government-backed lenders' standards they become non-warrantable. This means that buyers cannot get standard loans for these properties. They will have to pay cash or pay exorbitant rates through private lenders. When a building is full of non-warrantable condos, the pool of buyers shrinks and lowers the condo's value.

One might think that newer projects would have lower maintenance costs than older projects. But this isn't always true. Some builders set monthly fees low while they advertise the project. This attracts bargain buyers, but owners soon discover they have inadequate reserves. The monthly fees then skyrocket. Even if the homeowners successfully sue the builder, it is hard to sell any properties while litigation is pending, and values drop.

Most states have specific forms for condominium transactions in which the association discloses finances and reserves. Buyers must sign and verify they have examined the financial condition of the project. Pay attention to past history. How old is the roof? When were improvements last made? How often do association dues increase? Even though many people don't investigate these issues, a home's value depends on them.

CHAPTER 7

BANK FINANCING

*Banks have a new image. Now you have 'a friend,' your friendly banker.
If the banks are so friendly, how come they chain down the pens?*

— Alan King

Bank lending standards and terms change daily. This chapter provides general principles that should prove useful over the long term. We will examine how to borrow from banks to acquire or refinance a home. Please note the term "banks" as used here includes credit unions and other major financial institutions. There's another chapter on non-bank lending to help those who don't meet the criteria set by major lending institutions.

It may seem counterintuitive, but the lender is often not in charge of the loan process. Most bank loan programs are dictated by the government and financial markets. This is because home loans are usually packaged into bonds. In Wall Street terms, they are securitized. The loans are then sliced, diced, and traded. Thus, the person you deal with at the bank, and their superiors, may have very little ability to control the outcome of a loan decision.

The federal government helped start the largest buyers of home loans. These buyers include the Federal National Mortgage Association (FNMA, or Fannie Mae) and Federal Home Loan Mortgage Corporation (FHLMC, or Freddie Mac). The standards they set dominate the market and most loan programs follow their rules.

Many lenders will only make a loan if they can sell it to an investor. The value and terms of home-loan bonds change every day. This drives the constant fluctuations in the lending market. Ultimately, your home loan could be owned by a company halfway around the world from the bank that funded the purchase of your home.

Some lenders will keep your home loan in their own portfolio. This means that the lender can decide for itself whether you're creditworthy. If you fall outside the scope of Fannie and Freddie, look for financial institutions that keep their own loans. The best way to find these types of loans is through a savvy mortgage broker. You'll pay a broker a fee, and in exchange they will shop around and get you the best deal. A great real estate agent will help you find a reliable mortgage broker.

Key terms

Interest rates – Fixed vs. floating

Typically, the longer you lock in your interest rate, the higher the interest rate. Rates may rise during your loan term, so the lender wants to be compensated for that risk. The peace of mind that a fixed rate offers is worth a slightly higher interest rate for some. But others are willing to risk a floating rate, especially if they can afford to pay down the loan should rates become less favorable.

The right path depends on your overall financial picture. Neither a fixed nor floating loan is inherently better than the other. It's important to look at historical rates. If fixed rates are the lowest they've been in decades, lock them in if you plan to be in the home for many years. Alternatively, if you've got substantial investments you could liquidate in the event of a rate increase, floating rates may offer appealing savings.

Floating-rate loans are also called ARMs—Adjustable Rate Mortgages. This means the rate of the loan adjusts based on market conditions. ARMs can reset once a month or once every 10 years, depending on the loan program. The loan remains at the same interest rate between resets.

Loan programs use different methods to calculate the interest rate at reset. All loans reset based on an index and add some margin on top of that for the lender's profit. Most commonly, loans base the interest rate on LIBOR (London Inter-Bank Overnight Rate) or COFI (Cost of Funds Index). Historically, LIBOR is more volatile than COFI. Look at the historical fluctuations in both types before deciding which to choose. You can get an analysis of these indices from a mortgage broker or a financial advisor.

Few people stay in a home for 30 years. Locking in a fixed rate may not be best if you anticipate moving or selling an investment property in the short term. You may save money with an ARM if you plan to move again in five to seven years. On the other hand, if your plans change, you're at the mercy of the lending environment. Interest rates are usually limited as to how much they can move in any one year and capped as to how much they can move in total. Nevertheless, these jumps can be large and painful, even with caps.

Your real estate agent and mortgage broker can help you better understand the context of the lending environment. Your financial advisor can help you figure out if a fixed rate is ideal or if it makes more sense to go with an ARM. Ask questions, and *keep* asking questions until you understand and are comfortable with your choice. Those in the worst shape after the last financial crisis were those who had taken out loans they didn't understand.

Amortization – Fully amortizing, interest-only, balloon, negative amortizing

Amortization is the process of paying down the principal of the loan. Amortization can be complex and there are unlimited permutations. But the vast majority of residential loans fall into one of two categories: fully amortizing and interest-only.

Fully amortizing loans are the traditional and more common type of loan. The borrower repays the principal over the life of the loan. Each month you'll pay interest and a portion of the principal, so that the debt is zero in 30 years.

The downside is that the payments for fully amortizing loans are the highest. Since you're working to pay the debt down to zero, you pay part of the principal every month. To reduce the size of payments, lenders also offer interest-only loans, for which you pay only the interest.

Most interest-only loans will include a balloon payment where the entire principal is due. Five and ten year balloon payments are common. Very few people will have the cash to pay the bank at the time of the balloon. They expect to refinance into a new loan or to have moved by that time. But a balloon payment can be a problem if you cannot move or refinance. You'll want to ensure that the term includes some cushion. Get a balloon that becomes due in seven or ten years if you will be moving in five years.

People should pay off their loans at the optimal time. But theory rarely matches reality. It's common for people to owe as much when they sell their home or refinance it as they did on the day they bought it. An amortizing loan amounts to forced savings for some buyers.

APR

The APR (Annual Percentage Rate) is supposed to be a way to compare different loans. But it can be misleading. The APR is the total cost of the loan expressed as a percentage over the life of the loan. In theory, it includes all the fees such as appraisal and lender fees to provide an accurate picture of the real cost. Unfortunately, there's no standard for all lenders. One lender may leave something out of the calculation that another includes.

Note the APR calculation assumes you will pay the loan to its full maturity. That's 30 years for a fixed-rate loan. Very few people actually do this. The best loan will depend on your plans for the property. Look at the final numbers with your lender. The fact that you are now aware of this issue puts you in a better position than most loan applicants.

Prepayment penalties

Some loans charge you a fee to repay them early. If you were to sell the property, the lender charges you for not carrying the loan to maturity. These clauses are not present in most loans, but some do have them so it's important to inquire.

Assumable loans

There are loans that have assumption clauses built into them, meaning that they can be assumed by another borrower. This can be useful if it's a fixed-rate loan and rates have risen dramatically since the lender issued the loan. This can result in a higher sale price for the home. But the next borrower has to be approved by the lender. It's not worth great effort to secure a loan with this feature, but it is a bonus.

The above are the most common terms and negotiating points for bank financing. For additional terms, see the list in the Glossary. While it sounds obvious, it bears repeating: never take out a loan that you don't completely understand. Most lending horror stories start when people agree to loan terms they don't fundamentally understand.

CHAPTER 8

NON-BANK FINANCING

A bank is a place that will lend you money if you can prove that you don't need it.

— Bob Hope

What if you don't have the cash to buy a property, and the bank won't approve you for a loan? There are ways to finance a home that don't involve a bank, and they are much more viable than most people realize. Examine the options before limiting yourself to a rental.

Home sellers should also understand non-bank financing, as it can be a valuable tool in the sales process. Offering financing can expand the pool of potential buyers. Seller financing can get a sale done where other methods fail. Often the deal won't close with seller financing, but it does get more people in the door. Importantly, these methods can work at all price levels.

Whether buying or selling with seller financing, protect yourself by hiring an experienced agent and attorney. Non-bank financing introduces some additional complexity, so this is definitely not something to do on your own. The laws and regulations change frequently and vary from state to state. This chapter will give you enough information to ask the right questions, but is in no way a substitute for the services of professionals.

Seller financing may or may not be a right fit, but far too many people don't even consider it. Overlooking this powerful tool can cost people a great deal of money.

The carryback

The cleanest way to buy or sell a home without a bank loan is a seller carryback. In a seller carryback, the seller acts as the bank. At the close of escrow, the buyer gets clear title to the property, and the seller gets a promissory note. In other words, the buyer becomes the owner of the property, and the seller gets a note with the property serving as collateral.

Clear title means that the buyer's name is on the deed and is the owner of record. There are other ways to take ownership, or have an interest in a property, but they don't give the buyer clear title. We will review those later in the chapter. For now, know that the carryback is the best option as a buyer, if you can get it.

How does a carryback work? Here's an example: Joe Buyer wants to buy a house for $100,000 from Jane Seller. Joe only has $20,000 in the bank. Jane agrees to carry a note for $80,000. She will loan Joe the money with the house serving as collateral. The term of the note is 10 years and the rate is 7% interest, with no amortization (i.e. interest only). Joe must pay Jane $466.67 each month. After 10 years, Joe must pay Jane $80,000 with his own funds, or refinance the loan.

This is the best type of transaction for the buyer because the seller has no claim to the property after the close of escrow. It's as if the buyer bought with a bank loan; the ownership structure, rights, and responsibilities are the same as taking out a loan from a bank.

This process transforms the property into a passive income stream for the seller. Unlike owning a rental, there's no maintenance, taxes, insurance, or phone calls in the middle of the night. The seller must vet the buyer to make sure the buyer can handle the financial responsibility. The seller will also want a substantial down payment, to know the buyer has skin in the game. The agent and attorney will be essential throughout the process of structuring the deal, and a mortgage broker should review the buyer's financials.

Many sellers refuse to consider financing because they don't want to wait for their money. However, there is an entire industry of note buyers who will cash them out. Furthermore, often people sell their homes and wind up with the money sitting in a savings account or low-return investment. Keeping that money working for them in the property may be a smarter option.

Wraparound

A wraparound is a creative way to solve a limitation with carrybacks. If a seller already has debt on the property, she can't offer to carryback a note in the buyer's name and provide clear title at closing.

In a wraparound the buyer gets a carryback from the seller that is subject to the existing note on the property. The carryback from the seller is *wrapped around the existing* loan on the property.

What's the downside of the wraparound? At the close of escrow, the buyer's name will be on the title to the property, but the seller's name remains on the note. Thus, the seller's credit is still at risk if the buyer misses a payment.

Another impediment is the fact that most bank loans have a due on sale clause. If title changes, the note becomes due and payable immediately. However, these clauses are very rarely enforced. The banks tend not to ask questions when they are receiving payments on time. Nevertheless, the lender does have a right to demand payment in full. Banks might start enforcing these clauses if there are changes in the market that would make it advantageous to them.

In some states, it is not legal or practical to do a wraparound. As with all other methods in this chapter, speak to a real estate attorney.

Let's break it down with another example: Joe Buyer wants to pay $20,000 down for a $100,000 house. He wants a 10-year term and 7% interest rate with no amortization (i.e. interest only). Jane Seller owes $50,000 to Bank XYZ on her house at a rate of 5% due in 20 years. Joe will pay Jane $466.67 per month, and as part of her debt, Jane will pay $208.33 to the bank per month. Joe gets title to the property at the close of escrow. His payments are split so that $208.33 goes to Bank XYZ and the remaining goes to Jane. The note servicer or a title company typically handles this split.

Lease purchase (a.k.a. lease option, or rent to own)

A lease purchase—otherwise known as a lease option or a rent to own agreement—allows the buyer to have an interest in a property without full title. The buyer is a renter in the eyes of the law. The buyer has an option to become the owner by completing the purchase on terms to which the two parties have agreed.

This type of transaction is best for someone who doesn't have enough money for the down payment on a carryback, but expects to have sufficient funds to purchase in the foreseeable future. The buyer can get into the house now, and have a stake in it.

The downside is that the buyer's claim to title is weak. The option to purchase can be recorded with your local county recorder. But the buyer could be in the middle of a mess if the seller goes bankrupt, dies, or gets divorced. Buyers don't want to put too much money down for the option because of these risks. But sellers don't want to tie up their property without substantial money down. This tug-of-war can make these transactions difficult.

Hard money loans

Hard money loans are also called private money loans. In this type of loan, a private party serves as the lender. They are called hard money loans because the terms are hard: large down payments, high interest rates, and short repayment periods. Hard money lenders may have rates that are two to three times the bank rate, with larger down payments. Ouch!

Why would anyone choose a hard money loan? When the deal is too good to pass up, and even with high interest, the overall cost is compelling. Perhaps the tax advantages of owning a property outweigh the higher interest cost. A hard money loan may be a last resort, but it's important to know the option exists. Too many people think it's impossible for them to buy when that's simply not the case.

Land contract (a.k.a. contract for deed, installment sale, or agreement for sale)

Land contracts, usually reserved for land rather than houses, can be – but are not always – shady deals. Buyers should be on high alert if they encounter this type of deal. Land contracts often favor the seller instead of the buyer. Nevertheless, they can be a useful tool in some circumstances.

In a land contract, the buyer obtains equitable title, and the seller keeps legal title until the loan is fully paid. The buyer becomes responsible for all aspects of the property and is the owner as long as she honors the contract. If the buyer doesn't make timely payments, the seller can bring a forfeiture proceeding. Forfeiture proceedings do not have the same borrower protections as foreclosure proceedings. The seller typically gets her property back quicker and with less cost than a foreclosure process.

Not all states permit land contracts. Where permitted, they may be a helpful tool when used properly. All parties should consult experienced legal counsel.

CHAPTER 9

SELLING FOR TOP DOLLAR

When you cannot change what the product is, you have to change what it means.

— *Dan Kennedy*

You can't change the location of your home or the dynamics of the real estate market. But you can change how buyers perceive your home. Making the most of what you've got is the first step to selling your home. The second step is marketing your home, to get people in the door.

When it comes to improving how your home shows, the basics are the most critical, and yet often overlooked. Your home should look clean, bright, and functional. Not every home can be flooded with warm light, organized perfectly, and have an ideal layout. However, virtually every home can be cleaner, brighter, and better organized. It's astounding how many home sellers fail to address these basics, and it's costing them a fortune.

There is no single right way to prepare every home for sale. Rather, it depends on the market and your house. Position your property for the current market, and for the most likely type of buyer. Nobody intends to spend too much or too little on staging and improvements, and yet they often do. For example, there may be no reason to pay for improvements if you're in a market favoring fixer-uppers. Alternatively, it makes sense to spend money on staging and improvements if buyers are paying premiums for turnkey, move-in ready homes.

A real estate agent who's an expert in your area can be invaluable at this stage. She will tell you what's selling and *why*. Agents visit more properties than you'll ever see so they know what's a must-have and what's a deal breaker. They also know what the competition offers.

It's this competitive environment that's most important: your home doesn't have to be perfect, it just has to be better than the alternatives. For some homes, better means higher quality. For others, it means giving buyers a blank slate. Regardless of area or market conditions, to get top dollar, homes should be priced to market, staged well, and marketed thoroughly.

Selling your home yourself

On the surface, it may appear like "for sale by owner" (FSBO) can result in some savings. After all, if you're not paying a commission then that money should stay in your pocket. However, where theory and reality diverge is that mistakes can be costly, more than overwhelming the apparent savings. Even if everything goes off without a hitch, there's a huge time commitment involved in selling a home, and the value of your time should be factored into the decision.

Most FSBOs require large amounts of effort and time. To add insult to injury, the owners often lose money by selling their homes themselves. An amateur simply isn't going to get the same results as a professional. As the famous firefighter Red Adair remarked, "The only thing more expensive than hiring a professional is hiring an amateur."

If you think this opinion is biased since it comes from a real estate agent, here's a secret: the biggest fans of FSBOs are real estate investors. They absolutely love FSBOs because they're fertile ground for snagging bargains. Improperly marketed properties become stale, the owner gets exhausted, and along comes relief in the form of a much-reduced check. It's so lucrative for investors to buy FSBOs that there is a cottage industry to provide them with FSBO leads.

It's important to be aware of the things that can erase the apparent savings from a FSBO. For example, if you sell a house yourself instead of listing with a real estate agent, it looks like you'll save the value of the commission (e.g. 6% or whatever you choose to offer). However, that doesn't take into account the following factors:

- You will have fewer buyers looking at your property. Real estate agents cultivate buyers and advertise properties. Less demand equals a lower price and/or more time on market.

- You'll do all the work. There are a lot of moving parts in a real estate deal. The many hours you spend representing yourself are hours you won't spend at work or with your family.

- Most serious buyers are represented by an agent. Buyers' agents will want to be compensated. Thus, your commission savings may be cut in half.

- Negotiating for yourself can be dangerous. The person on the other side of the table may negotiate real estate deals every day. If FSBO's were generally well negotiated, real estate investors wouldn't swarm upon them like they do.

How to choose an agent

If you want to hire an agent to sell your home for you, there are some criteria you can use to get the best possible outcome.

1. *Choose the agent who will tell you the truth.*

There are two ways to price a home—at market value or with the "greater fool" theory. The former is based on research and data. The latter is based on the hope that a fool will come along and overpay. The most common refrain is that someone will fall in love with the home and *have* to have it. If you're serious about selling, it's unwise to list at the greater fool price.

Many sellers overestimate their home's worth, and it's understandable why. Everyone puts a lot of time and money into their homes, and their homes hold fond memories. But the market will establish a value for every home, and the market isn't sentimental. A competent agent will understand the factors involved in market dynamics, and clearly articulate them to you. Reconsider your expectations if the agent doesn't agree with your rose-tinted estimate, and has produced solid analysis to support their opinion of value.

Many agents do their clients a disservice by agreeing to list at an inflated price. They do that to land the listing, knowing full well that the property won't sell. Their expectation is that the seller will eventually reduce the price, and they'll be there to land the sale. However, that plan often fails and the home becomes stale on market. In the end, the seller has much more to lose than the agent.

Unscrupulous agents who agree to overprice homes make it difficult to know whom to trust. Here's a simple test to see if they're shooting straight with you: when they ask you how much you'd like for your home, throw out a price that's 25% higher than what you think your home is actually worth. If the agent accepts it without resistance, *run*. The agent is incompetent, or is willing to gamble with your money!

2. *Find someone who will market it vigorously.*

Hire the agent with a plan to not just list your home, but to get it sold. No agent can change market conditions, but by implementing a comprehensive marketing process, they can ensure your home gets the best possible exposure. Without a process, the outcome is left to chance – maybe your home gets the price it deserves, or maybe it doesn't.

Some agents will tout their ads in the local paper or the number of listings they have. Those things can help, but sometimes the top agent in an area takes a "play the odds" attitude about selling homes. That is, they list as many homes as possible, and yet many of their listings go unsold. You want someone who is committed to selling your home, not playing the odds with your financial future.

The best agent will have ongoing marketing to leverage for the benefit of your home. For example, extensive mailing lists are a great opportunity for your home to get exposure to serious buyers. If people are reading that agent's newsletter on a regular basis, then your home being showcased is a great opportunity. Blogs and social media can also be effective—if, and only if, people are paying attention and are responsive.

Ultimately, success comes down to hustle. Even the best plan or process fails if it's not followed enthusiastically. Sometimes technology does the trick, and a great sale happens quickly. Quite often, success comes from an agent picking up the phone, networking at events, and conveying genuine enthusiasm about your home. There's no substitute for hustle.

3.   Hire an experienced negotiator.

People respond to facts, data, and a clear presentation. An agent should be able to make a compelling, logical case for your position. Too often, agents simply relay terms without providing persuasive supporting information. In many cases the agent on the other side of the table wants to be able to persuade his/her client to take an offer, but they lack the ability to persuade their client. By giving the agent across the table the story behind your offer, and the supporting facts, you greatly enhance your chances of acceptance.

Some agents simply don't like to negotiate. Many agents are friendly and gregarious by nature, but those traits may work against them in negotiations. Choose an agent who enjoys and excels at negotiation, and knows when to dial down his or her personality. Ask about how many properties they've bought and sold for themselves. Also ask if they've had formal training in negotiation. If the agent is a real estate investor, and has been formally trained in negotiation, then you're likely in good hands.

It's also important that your agent has sold homes like yours. You don't want a person negotiating a $3 million sale if they've only negotiated $300,000 sales in the past. Their approach and expertise may not be suited to your target market.

Staging your home – the essentials

Staging can feel overwhelming, but the objective is simple: make it easy for someone to fall in love with your home. Prospective buyers should be able to envision the home as their own.

Assume that prospective buyers have no imagination. Don't make people imagine what a house *would* be if the paint wasn't chipped or the carpet wasn't stained. Buyers should feel like they are ready to move in that day. The exception would be if fixer-uppers and teardowns are selling well in your area; no point investing in staging if the buyer is looking for a blank canvas to paint her own picture.

Most people ask, "How much should I spend on staging?". This is the wrong question, and can lead to some poor decisions. Staging puts money in your pocket when done properly. A well-staged home sells quicker, and at a higher price. A poorly-staged home will linger on the market and sell at a lower price. The focus should be on determining what investments will reap the highest return.

Every home should be as clean and bright as possible; dirt and odor will always lower the price of any home. Invest in a professional cleaning. Clean the carpets if it has been more than six months since the last cleaning. Organize your clutter. If you're serious about selling, remove everything that you haven't used in the last six months and put it into storage. Your home will look larger, cleaner, and brighter.

If your home doesn't have abundant light, you can buy brighter, higher-quality light bulbs. This small investment can have a massive impact on perception of the property. All bulbs should be the highest wattage possible for each light fixture. Warm yellow light, mimicking the sun, is preferable to cool blue tones. When showing the house, open all window coverings for maximum light where there's no direct sunlight. Where there's direct sunlight at an undesirable angle, open blinds just enough to illuminate the room.

Beyond making a home as clean and bright as it can be, the next level of staging will depend on how you are marketing your home. If you anticipate that a buyer is going to want to remodel, you wouldn't make the same investments as if you were selling a turnkey dream home to suburban families. A good real estate agent will prevent you from wasting time and money on things that don't matter.

Staging your home – advanced

To ensure the fastest sale at the highest price, there are more steps you can take. Some of this requires you to invest considerably more, or to live differently than you may be used to. However, if you're serious about selling as quickly as possible for top dollar, then you'll want to consider these tactics.

De-personalize.

Your home is *your* home, full of memories and family photos. These personal items make it more difficult for prospective buyers to imagine the home as theirs. Religious and cultural decorations can also make it more difficult for prospective buyers to see themselves living in your home. Remove the highly personal touches, and make it easy for someone to imagine their belongings fitting right in.

Curb appeal.

You don't want a possible buyer's first impression to be negative. If your home has withering landscaping, patios that haven't been swept in ages, or sad-looking paint, you could get less for your home than you deserve. Little touches like a new welcome mat or outdoor furniture can also spruce up the appearance.

Inspect.

A buyer is likely to inspect and find things wrong with your home. Prevent surprises with your own inspection, and show that you've addressed any problems to comfort the buyer. The cost of an inspection is small and it allows you to get bids and have plenty of time to do repairs. Once you're in escrow, repairs may be rushed and costly.

Copy the professionals.

You can still learn from professional stagers even if you don't hire one. Look at the websites of home stagers in your area. They'll have plenty of "before" and "after" pictures. These pictures can give you a great understanding of how to transform a space.

Aroma

Las Vegas Casinos spend millions of dollars a year on the scents wafting through their buildings. Aroma can make people happier and more willing to spend money. Your entire home should smell wonderful. If you're not sure about what to buy, go to an expensive department store and check out their home department. Look for potpourri and scented candles, and don't be shy about asking for advice. If you're on a budget, go to an outlet mall where you'll find comparable items at a discount. The scent should be inviting and calm, not overpowering.

Marketing your home

Once your home is in peak form, the next step is getting people to see it. No showings mean no sales. While the MLS is a powerful tool for generating showings, we can greatly enhance its usefulness through effective marketing.

The sticking point with marketing is that word "effective"; effective marketing is what we want, but unfortunately a great deal of marketing is a waste of time and money. If you're using the services of an agent, the good news is in most cases they are paying those costs up front.

Nevertheless, if the agent is spending money on ineffective methods, you suffer since your house spends more time on market and sells for a lower price. This section isn't meant to make you an expert in marketing property, but it should help you ask the right questions and hire the best representation.

Photography is king

High-quality photographs are the most important asset in the sale of your home. Obvious, right? But many sellers simply don't get it. If you spend any length of time looking at home listings, you will undoubtedly see a home with pictures snapped on a smartphone. You may even see photos where they didn't bother to turn on the lights in the house. It's as if they are begging to have the home sit idle for months on end. Why this continues to happen is mystifying.

Here are the basics of what to do and what not to do to get the best photos of your home:

- **Pay a professional photographer.** Sure, smartphones have great cameras, but there's no substitute for the skills of an expert. Do not even consider skimping on this step; pay what it costs to get quality photographs taken.

- **Only hire a photographer with experience photographing homes.** Just because someone can take great pictures of your family or a landscape doesn't mean he or she can show your house in the best light. Hire someone who has the experience to know the best angles, what to show, and what not to show.

- **Schedule the shoot for mid-day.** No amount of photographic trickery is going to make a house photographed 30 minutes after sunrise look as bright and inviting as a home shot at 1 p.m. If you have to wait an extra day or two to get them scheduled at the right time, it will be worth the wait.

- **Check the weather forecast before scheduling the photo shoot.** Rainy or cloudy days are not your friend. If you see any sunny days in the 10-day forecast, wait to shoot. The photos are really important, so it's better to delay and get it right than be stuck with sub-par photos.

- **Get your home cleaned professionally the morning before the photo shoot.** And remember, it's not enough that everything sparkles; there should be no clutter as well.

- **Do not publish every photograph that's taken.** The job of the photos is to get people to want to come see the house. While this sounds obvious, people routinely make a mistake in direct contradiction to this principle. They feel compelled to include every photo that's taken, and flood the listing with images.

Any image that doesn't make people want to see the home should be omitted from the MLS and all advertising. If you have a guest bathroom that's a train wreck, just leave out that photo. Publish only the strong selling features and great photos; don't give people reasons to eliminate your home from consideration.

Beware of doing things "the way they've always been done"

For decades, the most common method of real estate advertising has been print media, such as newspapers and magazines. However common this practice may be, it does not mean it is effective. The real estate agents who have big pictures of *themselves* and their names in huge letters are selling themselves—not your home. Your home may have a portion of their ad, but they know—and the statistics prove—it's extremely unlikely to make a difference in selling your home.

To sell your home quickly, and for top dollar, go where the buyers are. The world has changed, and the statistics prove that homebuyers are *online*. Across all ages, areas, and income levels the trend is very clear. The days of people finding their next home in the newspaper are over. The serious buyers are looking online.

When advertising online, it's easy to target the ideal audience with great precision and minimal waste. For example, imagine that you're selling a $2 million property on a golf course. It's easy to target your ideal prospect and only your ideal prospect for maximum effectiveness. For example, target golfers with incomes over $500,000 who live in one specific zip code.

Another advantage of advertising online is that *your* home takes center stage, not the real estate agent. The feature is the house and its virtues, not the agent's smiling face.

The most common mistake made when listing a home is using sub-par photographs. This is usually the agent's fault. They are either skimping on paying for decent photos, or they haven't been honest with their seller about what's necessary to make the house show well. Sometimes it's a simple mistake, as when Mother Nature conspires against the photographer with a cloudy day.

The listing photos should reflect the best your home has ever looked. They can't necessarily make it look better than reality, but they should at the very least represent the best of reality. If the photos do not meet this standard, then get some more photos. Also, don't feel compelled to use every photo. If you have a bathroom that looks lousy no matter what, then don't include it in the listing. The photos should only provide reasons to see the property, not reasons to eliminate it from consideration.

Tried and true methods that still work

Technology is incredibly useful, but sometimes the simplest methods get the best results. Specifically, the best salespeople in the world may be your neighbors. People who live in the neighborhood are true believers, and they will represent it to others with great enthusiasm. But they cannot recommend what they don't know is available.

You should recruit neighbors to help you sell, particularly if you live in a tight knit community that shares amenities such as a golf course or clubhouse. People who know what makes that community special will best advocate to potential buyers. Talking to neighbors, sending postcards, and advertising in a neighborhood publication are simple, but still effective.

Similarly, it's important to tell friends and family that you're selling your home. The fond memories of times they've spent in your home help them see it in its best light. Everyone will run into *someone* who is moving, and you want your home to be at the front of your neighbor's mind.

Social media can represent the best of old and new methods. Fundamentally, it's about connecting with friends and family. But it's a lot more efficient and has wider reach than making phone calls. You'll get more value from social media posting if you make it entertaining. For example, don't just post "My house is for sale" and add a few photos. Instead, you could write a funny story about the 10,000 things you had to do to prepare for the shoot. Cleaning the clutter, rallying the kids, corralling the pets—these are all things people can relate to and laugh about. Stories like this make people more inclined to care about the fact you're selling your home and pay attention to those lovely photos.

Finally, there are some instances when print media can be worth the effort and investment. Specifically, when the home has very particular characteristics and the audience can be reached through a targeted publication. For example, if a luxury home has a 12 car air-conditioned garage, it's a safe bet the next buyer will be a serious car collector. Advertising in a local publication for auto enthusiasts would likely be money well spent. Two caveats to using print advertising are (1) the cost of the advertising should be justifiable relative to the exposure, and not just vanity advertising; and (2) the other advertising methods mentioned previously should have already been utilized.

CHAPTER 10

LET'S MAKE A DEAL

Everyone thinks they have good taste and a sense of humor.

— "When Harry Met Sally"

I've never met anyone who said he was a bad negotiator. Virtually everyone thinks they are above average, or even great, at negotiating. It's mathematically impossible for all of us to be above average at anything. The science of behavioral economics has proven that people tend to overestimate their abilities and prospects, and negotiation is no exception.

According to negotiation expert Herb Cohen, "In a negotiation, you want to care...*but not that much.*" The problem when you're negotiating for yourself: "not that much" is impossible. Herb has negotiated for US Presidents and Fortune 500 CEO's. Yet even he has hilarious stories of terrible negotiations in his own affairs, because his emotions ran amok. Even this world-class negotiator has botched his own real estate deals.

If an expert negotiator—someone who has consulted in hostage situations where lives were on the line—says not to negotiate for yourself, it's advice you should seriously consider. Our performance suffers as the level of emotion increases. Buying or selling a home is emotional. It's an important financial decision and impacts our family's lives. It's difficult not to take it personally. We are our own worst enemy during negotiations in which we are emotionally invested in the outcome.

Working with someone who has negotiated many millions of dollars worth of transactions can make the outcome better, and the process less stressful. An experienced negotiator knows the personal challenges involved. They can balance the emotional and financial sides of the transaction.

If you've followed this book's process for finding a great agent, you are well positioned for negotiations. After your goals have been clearly communicated, let your agent run the negotiations. Refrain from being a backseat driver. Without clear leadership, negotiations can go off the rails quickly.

Five critical elements of a successful negotiation

1. Know when to fold 'em – before the cards are dealt.

An effective negotiation starts with an effective decision. First determine what negotiating professionals call the BATNA. BATNA is an acronym for the Best Alternative To Negotiated Agreement. The concept is simple but powerful: if negotiations break down, what happens next? Without a clear picture *before* the negotiations start, it's difficult to know how long to stay at the negotiating table, and when to walk away.

In other words, what is your Plan B? If you don't have a BATNA before you start negotiating, your emotions take charge and you may not make the best decisions. Remove ambiguity, and reduce the impact of emotions, by agreeing to the BATNA before starting negotiations.

Imagine you've found a home that you love and can't live without, but it's outside of your budget. You can afford to stretch your budget, but is it the right choice? You're bound to face an emotional tug-of-war, especially if the seller won't come down in price. Decide up front what you'll do if negotiations don't go your way. Are there other comparable homes? Can you stay in your current home while you look again? Talk with your family and your agent, and put it in writing.

If you don't have anything to refer to, you may be impulsive in the negotiation. You don't have to write your BATNA in stone, but it's a starting point. You'll be able to look back see what you identified as the best alternative when you were not emotional. Something as simple as an email with a few bullet points will suffice.

2. *Gather intelligence.*

Once you've identified what's important, you can start figuring out how to get the best possible deal. Do your homework before negotiating. Identify your strengths and weaknesses, and those of the other party. Facts that may seem irrelevant in the beginning may be valuable in the future, so don't shy away from taking lots of notes.

Ask your agent to gather data on the real estate market and explain it to you. Automated online valuations, and even official appraisals, are often inaccurate. Your agent can access the most accurate data. She should also filter out irrelevant or misleading information.

Apart from the statistics, some detective work can shed light on what is happening in the life of the person on the other side of the table. The goal is to get a sense of their motivation beyond the numbers. All of us make decisions based on emotions, and those emotions can dramatically alter our decision-making. Any insight into what is happening on the other side of the table gives you an advantage during negotiations.

To gather intelligence on the other side, *repeatedly* ask open-ended questions. If you're a buyer, ask the seller why they are selling and where they are moving. Ask more than once because you are likely to hear different responses each time. This is particularly helpful when there are multiple people involved. For example, the seller may say one thing, their agent another, and the agent's assistant may yet reveal something else. It pays to talk to everyone.

3.   *There's one thing more important than money.*
Money is important, but so is time. And unlike money, once time is gone, it is lost forever. Time is critical in negotiations and is too often overlooked when crafting the negotiation strategy.

To know the relative strength or weakness of the buyer versus the seller, determine who has the greater time constraint. The one who is more rushed is in a weaker position. You can use this to your advantage.

If you're a buyer, determine how much time you have to secure your next home. What are the risks of a lengthy home search? If you're a seller, is there something pressuring you to move quickly, or can you take your time? In cases of both buyer and seller, do you think the market may move against you? Are interest rates likely to change unfavorably? These are some of the considerations to put time in its proper context for your negotiation.

Also consider the time the negotiation is likely to take. If buyer and seller are very far apart in their goals, there could be many rounds of counteroffers. Expecting a lengthy negotiation helps you prepare emotionally, and strategically determine your opening offer. Alternatively, if there is a constraint that limits the time for negotiation, your strategy may change.

4.   Don't look a gift horse in the mouth.

This old expression comes from the practice of inspecting horses by looking in their mouths. If a horse is given to you as a gift, the proverb tells you not to stand there and inspect it. Instead, smile and gratefully accept the horse.

In real estate, people sometimes get greedy once they get what they want. They reach their goal, and then they change their goal. This leads to perpetual dissatisfaction, trying to squeeze every last nickel out of every negotiation. Once you've reached your initial goal, any further negotiation is effectively looking the gift horse in the mouth. Every experienced agent can recount horror stories of great deals that were lost as a result of one party continually asking for "one more thing."

Know your ideal outcome before you start negotiations. If you get the sun and the moon, don't ask for the stars. If you've put your BATNA in writing, your agent and your family can help hold you to it. Don't jeopardize a great opportunity with unreasonable demands in excess of your original goals. Greed can be costly.

5. *Keep it simple.*

Albert Einstein opined, "Everything should be made as simple as possible, but not simpler." What is true in matters of science is true in real estate. Don't craft a complex offer with every conceivable contingency.

Begin negotiations with a clean and simple offer. An offer that's complicated may be rejected for that reason alone. Or it may put the other party on defense. Make it easy for the other party to understand your offer. They won't accept it if they don't understand it.

Most standard real estate contracts include contingencies for common issues. If you have unique circumstances or concerns, discuss them with your agent and attorney. Try to simplify the opening offer as much as possible. If circumstances require putting forth a complex offer, have your agent include a letter explaining the terms in plain English, and why they are important.

CHAPTER 11

CASE STUDY OF A COMPLEX TRANSACTION

Here lies Walter Fielding. He bought a house, and it killed him.

— *"The Money Pit"*

The following true story takes the previously covered concepts out of abstraction, and grounds them in reality. This case study includes surprises, heartburn, and outrageous personalities. It's a deal that would have died under most circumstances. This story demonstrates what's possible if you apply creativity and determination.

Your next home transaction is likely to be much easier than the tale below. However, if you run into problems, you can lean on the lessons in this case study. Specifically, this story shows how problems can become opportunities, as well as how to make the most of a committed and capable team.

Background

My client has stable income in the high six figures, but cannot qualify for a bank loan due to a foreclosure. Let's call him Tom. Tom sees real estate prices rising and wants to buy a home for his family before the market gets away from him. But he fears he will be stuck renting for years, since the banks won't lend to him.

I explain to Tom that he has more options than he realizes, and that I routinely help people with credit challenges buy luxury homes. Our options include seller financing and alternative lending programs. I encourage Tom to begin looking at homes despite his apprehension—after all, if we can't find him a home he wants, then financing is irrelevant.

Adding to the challenge, Tom *insists* on an architecturally significant mid-century modern home. The architecture is paramount above all other requirements. He would rather wait for an architecturally distinguished home to come on market than purchase another home more quickly. Homes of this quality and authenticity are quite rare, further compounding the complexity of the situation.

The Search

Tom begins receiving daily updates of homes in his area of interest, since it's a fast moving market. Architecturally significant homes sell especially quickly, so the daily update is important. He looks at everything and tells me what he likes and dislikes. I then adjust the search.

We look at properties when something is promising. But Tom's schedule is full and we often get to a property after it's already under contract. Other properties are asking prices that seem far too high to Tom. I assure him that I will negotiate aggressively on his behalf, but he is worried that he may already have missed the boat. We persevere, and keep tabs on the market.

The Home

A home that looks interesting falls out of escrow, and Tom and I run over immediately. Having looked at many homes and discussed architecture with Tom for years, I sense that we have found "it." The home is mid-century modern, heavily influenced by Japanese architecture. The landscaping integrates the Japanese theme brilliantly. The layout, flow, and interior/exterior synergy is extraordinary, with a spacious interior and a 2.2-acre lot.

However, the house itself is a disaster. It was built in the 1940s, and has been unoccupied for years. The last owner started to remodel but never finished. Some rooms have no flooring. There is a general sense of chaos pervading the house.

We open a cabinet to find a veritable treasure trove of architectural magazines from the 50s, 60s, and 70s—they are all tabbed, each one featuring this home or the architect who designed it. We have stumbled into a home of great significance, designed by one of Phoenix's great mid-century architects as his personal residence. As we dig deeper, we find a meticulous history of the home and the work performed on it. We've found decades of notes and invoices, neatly categorized in a file cabinet.

While the home had fallen into disrepair, it's clear that it had been loved. It's also clear this home is of great architectural significance. Tom "must" have it. His wife visits and falls in love with it, too. They're willing to put up with a big remodel to restore this home to its former glory.

This will be their family home for life, if we can make a deal.

The Challenge

The sellers are asking $1.1 million. This isn't remotely acceptable to Tom. The comparable sales don't justify their asking price, even if the home had been completely renovated. On the other hand, what is truly comparable when dealing with an architectural masterpiece? The sellers know the significance of the architecture, and that someone will pay a premium for it.

Since valuation will be more art than science, we lean heavier on the seller's position to base our strategy. I investigate the owners and their debt on the property. I ask lots of open-ended questions to gain insight into what the sellers might be willing to accept. They are cagey, but I confirm there is at least some willingness to negotiate.

Tom's wife is sitting out of the negotiation process, giving her proxy to her husband. I ask Tom what price for this would make him feel like he got a solid deal. Tom says, "If I could get this home for $750,000, it would be a no-brainer."

So here we are. The seller is asking $1.1 million. Tom wants to pay $750,000. They stand apart by a chasm of 32%. Plus, Tom needs financing to close this deal, which we haven't begun to arrange.

When two people are this far apart in their opinion of value, and the buyer doesn't even know if he can qualify for financing, most people would just walk away. Most people would call negotiation a waste of effort. To me, this situation sounds like a fun challenge.

No Financing, No Agreement, No Problem

Problem #1: We don't know how Tom is going to pay for this property. He has a high income, which should make things easier. However, like so many others, Tom took his lumps in the economic chaos of 2008. One thing is for sure: this won't be a cash deal, because my clients don't have sufficient funds at the moment. It also won't be a traditional bank deal because of the recent foreclosure.

Solution: I ask Tom about the details of his foreclosure, and determined that the foreclosure should no longer impact Tom's ability to get a bank loan by January 2013. We found the home in summer 2012. If we are to close in 60 to 90 days, that's a 6-month gap. We could ask for a longer close, or bring in hard money to ensure that Tom doesn't lose his dream home.

Problem #2: Buyer and seller are separated by over 30% in their desired price for the property. Because this is such an architecturally significant house, it's impossible to come up with directly relevant comparable sales data. I put forward comps to support my client's position, and the seller will do the same. Because there are no other homes like this one, valuation is more art than science.

Solution: The ambiguity of the numbers may work to our advantage, if we apply a methodical negotiation process.

We produce documentation to justify our position, and after a series of tense exchanges, we get the price down to a little over $900,000. It's a $200,000 reduction, but is still more than Tom wants to pay. The seller won't budge any further, so it became necessary to pull a rabbit out of the hat, so to speak.

While the negotiations on the house had been underway, I simultaneously undertook a second set of negotiations. I crafted a deal for Tom to sell one acre of this 2.2-acre property, after he consummated his purchase. The house and yard on 1.2 acres are enough for Tom. That one acre will bring in $350,000. This means Tom will get the house on 1.2 acres for just $600,000. That's $150,000 less than his dream price of $750,000!

We demand that the buyer of the land put down a $100,000 earnest deposit that would be non-refundable. Thus, if the land buyer defaults, Tom keeps that $100,000. In that situation, Tom's basis in the property would be $800,000. He could then find another buyer for the land. This is a slam-dunk for Tom!

Or so we thought...

Problem #3: We all know that an appraiser is going to have a heck of a time valuing this unique home. So even if I can get Tom qualified by an alternative lender, the deal may fall apart.

Solution: To avoid appraisal problems, we're left with seller financing as our best option. We don't know that the seller will grant it, but it's a legitimate solution. The seller must be aware of the difficulty an appraiser would have valuing the home.

The higher the price of the property, the more likely there's a well-heeled seller who can afford to carry a note. Given that this valuable property has been sitting vacant and costing the sellers money for quite some time, I'm optimistic the odds are with us.

Problem #4: Tom is freaking out. The combination of uncertainty and desire is taking its toll. He "knows" the deal is dead and is lamenting the loss. "We're asking for so many things, Alex," he moans. "We're so far apart that this will never work! I don't want to waste your time, this will never work!"

Solution: I assuage Tom's concerns. "Listen, Tom, we're not going to come at them with everything all at once. We prioritize, strategically introduce deal points, and solve one problem at a time. If you throw a frog into boiling water it jumps right out, but if you put it in cold water and let the water boil slowly, the frog gets cooked." He laughs. I also assure him that he isn't wasting my time. "I live for this, Tom," I say. "If I didn't need to work, I'd still do this for free."

Problem #5: The seller had previously sold a home with seller financing and it did not end well. The seller had to foreclose, and is determined to never, ever "make that mistake" again. Never!

Solution: I highlight the fact that we're only asking to finance for six months, and that my client is a stable family man who doesn't want to move his family around. He has a long history of superb income. And the seller will get $150,000 in cash at closing. The seller eventually backs off the "Never!" posture.

Problem #6: It comes to light that Tom was actually one year off from the foreclosure date he provided, so he is farther away from bank financing than we thought. That extra year makes our request now more than temporary financing, and raises all the concerns the seller originally had. The seller says he is no longer comfortable with carrying the note for any length of time Game over?

Solution: First, take a deep breath. So the seller no longer will carry, which appears to make the deal go bust. I have vetted lenders that offer financing to people with credit challenges. It took considerable work to find one offering reasonable rates. I've had to "kiss a lot of frogs" to find the prince that will deliver for my client. Fortunately, now I've got a reliable source to ensure that the perfect home won't escape from my client. Their rate will be higher than most lenders, but this deal is so good Tom doesn't want to lose it.

I discuss values with the lender to ensure that they are on board, and while "it ain't over 'til it's over," we are making progress. The lender likes the fact that we're selling the land and will reduce the size of the loan early on, and they are savvy enough to understand the transaction. Score!

Problem #7: The seller announces that he wants to sell the acre of land themselves, rather than letting Tom do it after the close of escrow.

Solution: We are all unnerved by the change, there have been so many twists and turns one more could break apart everything. When cooler heads prevail, we realize that as long as the purchase price pencils out no higher for Tom, this would be a much better structure for Tom not to have to deal with selling the land. A lower initial purchase price means it's easier to get lender approval, less interest cost, and fewer moving parts to the transaction. All I have to do is make sure that Tom pays the same price for the house he would have paid if he had sold the land himself.

Problem #8: The seller's agent has told us to "take it or leave it." They want to sell the land themselves, or the deal is off.

Solution: Even though this new structure could actually benefit Tom, the seller's agent did a terrible job of selling it to us. He took a very aggressive, egocentric attitude rather than collaborating to solve a problem. He wasn't thinking through our wants or needs and trying to address them; he was trying to grind it out, to be tough.

Their terms did indeed make this a better deal for Tom. Nevertheless, rather than just accepting the new terms, we create a paper tiger just in case we needed leverage for any future possible bumps in the road. We threaten to walk away if they try to change the deal. Why would we do this when the new deal was even better for Tom? Because there have been so many twists and turns in this deal, that I want to make sure we keep some powder dry in the event there's another problem.

If it looks like we are giving them something, rather than them giving us something, we have leverage to negotiate as needed. But if we took this as a gift—which it was in reality—we would be out of ammo, so to speak. If the seller's agent had spent more time trying to see things from our point of view, he could have presented this as the gift it was. Instead, he tried to play tough guy when there was no reason to do so, and so we responded in kind.

We ultimately lock up the deal, and the net price to Tom is even lower than the original deal of buying the house and selling the excess acre. The extra savings comes from the fact that Tom isn't on the hook for closing costs on the land sale. The new price? $579,000. That's almost 50% less than the original asking price, and $171,000 less than Tom's "dream price."

Conclusion

Tom closes on his dream home for $579,000. When we started, his "no brainer" goal was $750,000. We negotiated almost 50% off the asking price. The only thing that Tom didn't get was an acre of land he didn't particularly want—the 1.2 acres he kept was more than sufficient for his kids to play, and for his wife to have a wonderful garden. The alternative lender financed Tom at just 2% above the cost of bank financing with only 20% down. In sum, Tom got his dream house, a true architectural gem that he can restore to its full glory and live in for the rest of his life.

As we toured the home right before closing, Tom's wife said to me as Tom nodded, "This deal would never, ever in a million years have happened without you, Alex. We couldn't be more thrilled." I have never been more proud, honored, and delighted in my professional life.

Whenever somebody says a deal is dead, I remember this story. As Thomas Edison said, "When you have exhausted all possibilities, remember this: you haven't."

Postscript

1. Do you really go to these lengths on every deal, or was this just a one-in-a-million situation?

It's not always necessary, nor advisable, to have such complex negotiations. At some point, the best negotiation strategy is to stop negotiating. Knowing when to stop, and when to keep going, is the most valuable skill learned through experience. Regardless of whether one expects complex negotiations or not, it is wise to prepare as if they will be lengthy and complex.

The best analogy to negotiation is litigation. The very best litigators settle their cases advantageously for their clients without setting foot in court. But they are ready for court, should the need arise. It's my goal as a negotiator to get a great deal for my client as quickly and painlessly as possible. If negotiations get tricky, though, I'm prepared.

2. Is seller financing available even in a seller's market?

Market conditions will certainly impact the number of available opportunities for seller financing. However, it only takes one seller and one buyer to make a deal.

Even in a hot market, there may be a seller who has no plans for the money they'll receive upon the sale of their property. In such a case, financing the sale is solving a problem for the seller—they now have a plan for their money, paying them monthly income, and total confidence in the collateral. Alternatively, a buyer may have a bank willing to fund 90% of the agreed upon purchase price; the seller financing that final 10% may be a better option for them than losing the deal.

Thus, even in red hot markets where buyers are scrambling to find homes, seller financing can and does happen.

CHAPTER 12

CONTRACTS AND CLOSING COSTS

Education is when you read the fine print.
Experience is what you get if you don't.

— *Pete Seeger*

When people are excited about buying or selling a home, they may be tempted to skim the contracts. The details are boring when you're dreaming of life in your new home. However, it's critical to understand the basics *before* the contract is in front of you.

Once you receive a contract, you are under the pressure of a deadline to respond. That's not an ideal circumstance to learn. It's wise to invest time to understand the process in advance, so you're not trying to figure it out when time is of the essence.

The form of the contract will vary from state to state, and even city to city. This chapter isn't meant as legal advice, or as a substitute for the services of a real estate agent. However, it will get you familiar with the core elements common to virtually all real estate contracts.

Parties

The names of the buyer and seller who are party to the contract.

Legal description and property address

Legal description and property address

The legal description is how a surveyor describes the property, whereas the address is how the Postal Service and everyone else refers to it. It's crucial that the legal description be accurate. This is especially important when purchasing land. A survey may be attached to the contract to clarify what precisely is being sold.

Purchase price

This is the proposed purchase price offered by the buyer. It is subject to change until both buyer and seller have agreed.

Earnest money (a.k.a. earnest deposit)

Earnest money is the funds the buyer must put into escrow to show "earnest intent." If the buyer doesn't fulfill his commitments under the contract, this money typically goes to the seller. The seller may also be able to sue the buyer for breach of contract; buyers should be aware whether they have additional risk beyond the earnest deposit.

Down payment

The down payment is the cash the buyer commits toward the purchase of the home. For example, if the lender will loan 80% of the purchase price, then the down payment will be 20%. The funds due at closing will be this 20%, less any earnest money already deposited, plus closing costs.

Financing

The buyer must disclose details of how she intends to fund the purchase. If it's a cash deal, then she must provide proof of funds to the seller. When using financing, she'll need to disclose the type of financing, the name of the lender, and all relevant details about the loan. The seller has a right to know that legitimate financing backs the offer.

Contingencies

The contingencies are escape clauses that allow one or both parties to exit the contract upon specific conditions. The most common contingencies are inspection and financing. If the buyer is unsatisfied with the home during the inspection period, she can walk away without sacrificing her earnest deposit. And if the financing falls through, the buyer may also cancel the contract. Possible contingencies are as vast as the imagination. Talk to your agent and attorney if you don't understand the contingencies. Numerous contingencies are a warning sign that the transaction is unlikely to close.

Expiration

The date by which the offer must be accepted before it expires. It is common for parties to request a response within 24 to 48 hours. If an offer is not accepted by both parties prior to expiration, it becomes non-binding.

Disclosures

Sellers are required to disclose certain facts about the property. The specific disclosures required vary by region. Generally, the seller should disclose anything that materially impacts the value of the property. Failure to properly disclose is one of the most common causes of litigation. Hence, sellers should take this responsibility seriously.

Personal property

Personal property such as appliances and furniture may be incorporated in the transaction. There is generally a section of the contract that will specify these items. It's important to note that lenders will often take issue with personal property being part of the purchase contract. The lender is leading on the value of the real estate, not furniture or artwork, and so lenders demand the transaction of personal property be handled separately. In cash transactions, personal property can generally be included in the real estate purchase contract if both parties wish.

Escrow

The escrow company is the neutral third party who will hold all funds and transfer title. The escrow company will often issue a title insurance policy too. However, in some states attorneys handle the escrow, and a title insurance company underwrites the policy.

Prorations, assessments, and fees

This part of the contract deals with the split between the buyer and seller for items like property taxes, homeowners' association assessments, home warranty, lender fees, and escrow fees. There is usually a customary split. Of course, it's always open to negotiation. In some circumstances, such as with homeowners' association transfer fees, the amounts may be substantial.

Closing date

The closing date is when the funds will pass to the seller and title will be recorded in the name of the buyer. This can be an important point of negotiation if the buyer has to move out of his old residence by a particular date or if the seller needs additional time to accommodate her move. Avoid closing on a Friday; if there's a delay, you'll be stuck until Monday.

Risk of loss or damage

There will usually be a clause pertaining to damage to the property during escrow and what will happen if there is a catastrophic loss. The seller is usually responsible for repairing damage. However, this can be impractical beyond a certain level and nullify the deal. For example, if a house burns down five days before closing, the seller isn't going to be able to rebuild the house in time for closing. In such extreme cases, many contracts would call for the contract to be cancelled, and the earnest deposit to be returned to the buyer.

Dispute resolution

Many contracts outline a procedure for resolving disputes should they arise. Your attorney can advise you about the best way to protect your interests. If you do not see any dispute resolution clause, it may be worth inquiring about why it is absent.

Signatures and effective date

The contract has no legal force until all parties have signed it. The date when the last signature is made becomes the effective date of the contract. Some contingencies, such as the inspection period, are based on the effective date. Thus, a delay in signing can have a domino effect impacting the timeline of the transaction.

Shedding light on closing costs

Everyone knows there will be closing costs, but they're usually unclear until the transaction is well under way. Closing costs can still be substantial. Transactions involving loans are more expensive and complex than cash transactions. If you use a loan, you'll want to understand the fine print. All lenders provide a summary of costs in the form of the Loan Estimate and Closing Disclosure. These documents are the buyer's primary resources for understanding costs.

Below is a table showing the customary allocations to the parties depending on the type of financing. You may negotiate different terms and there may be some regional variations, but this chart is still a good starting point.

A blank cell indicates there is no industry-wide customary split. These costs can be negotiated, although some are too minor to bother. Your escrow officer may have a customary split and it's worth inquiring about fees early on in the process. Note that the customary split differs depending on financing. Some loan types actually require a certain split, and if a contract conflicts with that requirement, either the contract or the loan must be changed.

CLOSING COSTS: WHO PAYS WHAT

	CASH	FHA	VA	CONV
Down payment	BUYER	BUYER	BUYER	BUYER
Termite inspection	*	*	SELLER	*
Property inspection	BUYER	BUYER	BUYER	BUYER
New loan origination fee	*	BUYER	BUYER	BUYER
Loan discount points	*	BUYER	SELLER	BUYER
Document preparation fee	*	SELLER	SELLER	BUYER
Credit report	*	BUYER	BUYER	BUYER
Appraisal or extension fee	*	BUYER	BUYER	BUYER
Existing loan pay-off	SELLER	SELLER	SELLER	SELLER
Existing loan pay-off demand	SELLER	SELLER	SELLER	SELLER
Loan prepayment penalty	SELLER	SELLER	SELLER	SELLER
Prepaid interest (approx. 30 days)	*	BUYER	BUYER	BUYER
Mortgage transfer fee	*	*	*	*
Reserve account balance (credit seller/charge buyer)	*	PRORATE	PRORATE	PRORATE
FHA mortgage insurance premium, VA funding fee, private mortgage insurance premium	*	BUYER	BUYER	BUYER
Assessments (sewer, paving, etc.)	SELLER	*	*	*
Property taxes	PRORATE	PRORATE	PRORATE	PRORATE
Tax impounds	*	BUYER	BUYER	BUYER
Tax service contract	*	SELLER	SELLER	BUYER
Fire/hazard insurance	BUYER	BUYER	BUYER	BUYER
Flood insurance	*	BUYER	BUYER	BUYER
Homeowners' association (HOA) transfer fee	SPLIT	SPLIT	SELLER	SPLIT
HOA disclosure fee	SELLER	SELLER	SELLER	SELLER
Current HOA payment	PRORATE	PRORATE	PRORATE	PRORATE

Next month's HOA payment	BUYER	BUYER	BUYER	BUYER
Home warranty premium (negotiable)	*	*	*	*
Real estate agent commissions	SELLER	SELLER	SELLER	SELLER
Homeowner's title policy	SELLER	SELLER	SELLER	SELLER
Lender's title policy and endorsements	*	BUYER	BUYER	BUYER
Account servicing set-up fee	*	*	*	*
Escrow fee (NOTE: Charge seller on VA loan)	SPLIT	SPLIT	SELLER	SPLIT
Recording fees (flat rate)	SPLIT	SPLIT	SPLIT	SPLIT
Reconveyance/satisfaction fee	SELLER	SELLER	SELLER	SELLER
Courier/express mail fees	SPLIT	SPLIT	SELLER	SPLIT
Wire fees	SPLIT	SPLIT	SELLER	SPLIT
Email of loan documents	*	BUYER	SELLER	BUYER

*Blank boxes indicate there is not usually a customary split, and this cost is usually negotiated in the purchase contract.
FHA: Federal Housing Administration loan
VA: Veterans Administration loan
CONV: conventional loan

CHAPTER 13

REAL ESTATE CLOSINGS STEP BY STEP

No matter how great the talent or efforts, some things just take time.
You can't produce a baby in one month by getting nine women pregnant.

— Warren Buffett

Negotiating a deal is serious work, often fraught with emotion. But reaching agreement and signing the contract is just the beginning of the process. There are many steps between signing the deal and exchanging the keys, and most people are unclear on how they work. Here's a comprehensive guide, so you'll know what to expect.

Step 1: Earnest deposit

The buyer will first need to deposit funds into escrow to show "earnest intent" (i.e. good faith). The contract is tentative until the deposit enters escrow. The contract will specify the amount and deadline for the deposit. The seller can usually cancel the deal if the earnest deposit is late. Thus, the buyer should put the earnest deposit into escrow immediately after signing the final contract.

The amount of earnest money will depend on the purchase price, usually one to five percent. In some markets, the standard earnest deposit may be higher. The larger the earnest money deposit, the more seriousness the buyer conveys to the seller.

The earnest money is placed into an escrow account and held there until closing. At closing, the funds are applied against the purchase price. For example, if you buy a $1 million home and put down an earnest deposit of $25,000, you'd be required to pay the seller $975,000 at closing.

Most buyers want to know if they are at risk of losing the earnest money. The answer is yes, if you break the terms of the contract. The contract should cover relevant contingencies, and protect the buyer's deposit if the house does not pass due diligence. Always review the contingencies, and make sure you mark your calendar with all deadlines. Failing to meet contingencies or letting deadlines slip by can put the earnest deposit at risk.

Step 2: Seller property disclosure and CLUE report

Sellers must disclose material details about the condition of their property. Specific disclosure requirements vary by state. A leading cause of litigation is inadequate disclosure; thus sellers should disclose as much as possible. Buyers should lean on their real estate agent if the disclosures seem inadequate or confusing. Buyers should also perform their own diligence to avoid surprises. Meet the neighbors and do some Internet sleuthing about the area.

The buyer will also receive a CLUE (Comprehensive Loss Underwriting Exchange) report that shows the home's recent insurance loss history. This comes from an independent third party. It can give you information on the safety of the neighborhood. For example, it identifies how many robbery claims were paid in the past two years. Insurance claims over the past five years can impact the buyer's insurance premiums after you buy the home. The best CLUE report is an empty one, with no recent claims.

Share the disclosures and CLUE report with your inspector. While the home inspector's job is to find problems, providing this information reduces the chance of missing something important.

Step 3: Inspections

Once the buyer's earnest money is in escrow, it's time to inspect the property. This is crucial to protect the buyer. If the inspector finds a serious problem that the seller is not willing or able to address, the buyer does not have to consummate the purchase and can recover their earnest money.

A certified inspector should conduct the inspection. They will provide the buyer with a detailed report of the property's condition. A buyer might rethink their decision to buy a home if the inspector finds, for example, structural damage that would require $25,000 to repair. The buyer may choose to reject the premises and cancel the contract. Alternatively, the buyer can ask the seller to repair the damage. The seller can respond in one of three ways: agree to repairs, offer a credit so the buyer can conduct the repairs, or refuse any repair or credit and let the buyer out of the contract.

An important caveat regarding a credit at closing is that some lenders will limit the amount. If a buyer plans to accept a large credit instead of a major repair, they should clear it with the lender. It may be possible to decrease the sales price as an acceptable alternative to a credit at closing.

If the buyer and seller disagree about repairs during the inspection period, the buyer can generally choose to walk away from the contract with their earnest deposit. But every contract is different, so pay close attention to the inspection clause, especially since there's usually a time limit.

The home inspection can take up to a full day depending on the home's size and age. The buyer does not have to be present for the entire inspection. It's best to give the inspector space to do her thing. You can review the report and discuss any crucial findings at the end.

Most inspectors will find something wrong with virtually every home. Don't be alarmed. The list may be long and intimidating, but most issues will be minor or cosmetic. Rely on your inspector and agent to help determine what may be a minor inconvenience, an expensive but manageable repair, or a potential ongoing headache.

You many need to supplement the general home inspection with specialized inspections. If there is evidence of water damage, you should get a mold inspection. If there is a plumbing or electrical issue, ask a specialist to determine the full extent of the problem. Given the potential for follow-up inspections, the buyer should begin the general inspection as early as possible.

Step 4: Title report

A clear title means that no one has a competing legal claim to the property that could stop a sale. The title company will conduct a title search to confirm this. A title search is a careful review of legal records to ensure that the seller can convey the home can to the buyer at the close of escrow. The officer will look for liens, bankruptcies, or judgments against the property, as well as back taxes.

A clear title means that the seller can transfer it to the buyer without any problems. If there is a cloud on the title, the seller cannot sell until the cloud is resolved. Examples of such clouds, or title defects, include:

- liens or encumbrances, such as debts to contractors or unpaid taxes;
- failure to properly record or file documents in past real estate transactions;
- improperly constructed documents used in prior transactions.

If a search uncovers any of these problems, the escrow officer's title department will determine whether it can locate the parties involved and lift the cloud.

The title report may reveal other facts that that can affect a buyer's decision to buy the property. There may be an easement on the property, for example. An easement is permission for someone else to access certain parts of the property, such as a driveway easement for a neighbor. The easement may not be visible, but it can affect the property and its value.

Presuming there are no deal breakers in the title report, a title insurance policy will be issued to the buyer at closing. The lender, if any, will also get a title insurance policy. This policy will cover any future claims on the title based on claims that may have been missed during the title search. While claims against title are uncommon, especially in urban and suburban settings, they can arise.

Step 5: Money

Soon after opening escrow, all parties will receive a preliminary settlement statement. This will outline closing costs and specify how all funds will be disbursed at closing. This document accounts for every penny. It is subject to change over the course of the escrow, so be sure to have the latest version in hand at any given time. As the closing date nears, a final settlement statement will be issued. This statement will show exactly how much money the buyer needs to have at the closing to finalize the purchase.

The buyer must have already placed the funds in escrow and settle any existing liens on the property on the closing day. In cash deals the buyer simply wires the funds to the seller. There will be some paperwork involved if the buyer is using financing, but the parties have already done most of the work.

Transactions can fall apart late in the game when banks are involved. The buyer should have a Plan B so the transaction can proceed if the primary lender pulls out. It's also important to respond quickly to any of the lender's requests.

Banks are notorious for taking a long time to review documents. Yet they are prone to demand large amounts of information at a moment's notice. Plan for this unfair reality, be organized and responsive. There's only so much a real estate agent can do for you in this arena, since it involves personal financial information. The buyer should plan to proactively communicate with the lender throughout escrow, to ensure no problems arise at the 11th hour.

The bank should order an appraisal as soon as inspections are complete and the buyer confirms her intent to close on the property. Without an appraisal the whole lending process stops.

If you don't receive an appraisal date within a few days after your inspection period, call the lender. Your agent will arrange for the appraiser to have access to the property.

Step 6: Home warranty, property insurance, and utilities

Home warranties cover appliances and systems in the home for a set duration, usually one year. This provides protection if something stops working in the first few months. In many home transactions, the seller pays for the home warranty. Even if the home seller doesn't offer it, buyers often purchase it for peace of mind.

Home warranties have serious limitations, so do not consider this protection any reason to skimp on inspections. They operate like insurance policies with limits and deductibles. That deductible generally takes the form of a fee you must pay to have a worker come to your home. The limits and fees associated with home warranties vary greatly, as do their levels of customer service. Ask your real estate agent for recommendations.

The warranty will generally cover repairs on major systems and appliances. Warranty coverage varies but typically includes:

• Kitchen appliances
• Heating and air conditioning
• Electrical systems
• Ceiling and exhaust fans
• Plumbing
• Water heaters
• Pools

Most warranties don't cover roofs. Roof riders usually have low limits. Roof problems are common and expensive, so the economics don't support comprehensive insurance coverage. Careful inspection of the roof is essential.

You must also get insurance coverage before moving into the home. The buyer will want full insurance coverage on the home the moment they receive the keys to protect his investment, and the lender will require proof of insurance.

Before the final walkthrough and closing, the buyer will need to set up the utilities. The seller will provide a list of utility companies, so the buyer can pick up where they leave off. Some utility companies are notorious for long delays in setting up new accounts, so contact them early.

Step 7: Final walkthrough

The final walkthrough is an important protection for the buyer. Most sellers will take care of their homes until they move out. But the buyer should always verify the condition. The walkthrough gives the buyer the chance to inspect for any changes in the condition of the home during escrow.

Consider as an example a seller who has to short-sell a home because he can no longer afford it. This seller won't make any money, and thus he may not be motivated to keep the home in good repair. If the movers damage the drywall in the living room, the seller may not fix it, and the buyer gets the house not in the expected condition but in shambles.

The walkthrough should be a few days before the closing date after the seller moves. The seller may walk through and explain some of the home's features. The most important function of the walkthrough is to confirm that the home is in the same condition as when the buyer agreed to purchase it.

Step 8: Funding, recording, and the close of escrow

In the final step, all funds are exchanged and title passes to the buyer. The change in title is recorded with the local government, making the change of ownership official.

The paperwork involved varies by state. In many states, lawyers will represent the buyer and seller. In other states, lawyers are rarely involved. Ask your agent at the beginning so you'll know what to expect. And if you do choose to hire a lawyer during this process, ask someone you trust to refer you to an attorney.

The transaction is complete once all documents are recorded. The seller will give the keys to the buyer. The buyer should still hire a locksmith; for a modest fee you'll have peace of mind that you're the only one who can access the property.

Conclusion

There are a lot of people, documents, and transfers involved in closing a real estate transaction. Your real estate agent's role is to coordinate the people involved to ensure a smooth closing. Set your expectations with your agent early. Some people want a weekly update, others may want to know every detail as it happens. If you and your agent establish a clear standard of communication, you should enjoy an easy closing.

CHAPTER 14

THE BASICS OF REAL ESTATE INVESTING

Investing should be more like watching paint dry or watching grass grow. If you want excitement, take $800 and go to Las Vegas.

— Paul Samuelson, Nobel Prize Winner in Economics

Many people see real estate as a safe alternative to riskier investments. The logic is simple: people will always need a place to live. Values may fluctuate, however they will never go to zero.

But it's not that simple. Real estate is a multi-trillion dollar industry and there are many ways to invest. New investors are often unaware of the legal and tax consequences of real estate investments. From the responsibilities of landlords, to the tax benefits of 1031 exchanges, there's a lot to know.

We'll cover some of the common mistakes new investors make and how to decide what investment is right for you. We're focusing on residential real estate, since it's the first place that most new investors turn. Commercial real estate typically requires more capital and more specialized knowledge.

Top five mistakes of new real estate investors

1. Short-term thinking

Real estate is a steady long-term investment, consistently delivering appreciation and cash flow. The key phrase there is *long-term*. Real estate markets can change dramatically over just a few months. This can be a problem if you need to sell. A real estate investment is like a bank Certificate of Deposit (CD) in one respect: there may be a penalty for early withdrawal. That penalty can be quite severe in real estate when selling at the wrong time.

Plan to hold onto a real estate investment for five ten to years, or longer. If your time horizon is less than five years, you may be taking a big risk. In the wise words of Warren Buffett: "Our favorite holding period is forever."

2. Excessive leverage

Leverage is a great multiplier of results. It multiplies both bad results and good results. In a down market, leverage can undo the greatest fortunes. When you read about a billionaire who is suddenly bankrupt, the reason is almost always excessive leverage.

So what is leverage? Simply put, it's the effect of debt. Imagine that investment properties are selling for $200,000. If you borrow 75% of the price, you get four-to-one leverage. In other words, a $200,000 investment can buy four homes instead of one. You use the $200,000 to deposit 25% on each property, instead of one outright purchase.

In a rising market the person who takes $200,000 and leverages it to buy four or five properties looks like a genius. Their accumulated gains are massive. The conservative person who paid cash and owns just one property looks like a bore. Of course, when the market changes the roles reverse: if rents go down and do not cover the costs of the property, or if interest rates rise, the leveraged owner may encounter catastrophic problems.

People who take on leverage are betting they can hold long enough, or precisely time the sale of the properties, to take advantage of the market. Some people will be fortunate enough to do this. Many will not. It gets ugly when everyone runs for the exit. But you won't be forced to sell if you've paid $200,000 in cash. And you won't be forced to sell low if you lose a tenant or interest rates rise. Your property may lose value and your rental income may decrease, but it will not be catastrophic.

To determine how much leverage is right for you, figure out what type of a return you need. If your financial plan calls for a 6% return to ensure a comfortable retirement and you can achieve that return without any leverage, then don't leverage. If you choose to increase your returns with leverage, lock in the rate to ensure your mortgage payment won't change when rates rise.

3. Insufficient research

You must perform all the due diligence for an investment property that you would for your personal residence, and more, if you want your investment to be profitable and stress-free.

First, understand the rental market. Investigate the current average rent, the trends, and the competition. How does your prospective property compare to specific nearby rental properties?

You must also understand the area's employment situation. Are new companies moving in? Or is a major employer leaving? Are incomes rising or falling? Changes in the area's employment and income status affect property values and rental rates. Do your homework to avoid unpleasant surprises. This is where leaning on an expert is critical: to know what questions to ask, and what facts you may have overlooked.

4. Not establishing solid professional relationships

Successful investors use the help of professionals. You will likely need a property manager and contractors for maintenance and repairs. An accountant who understands real estate is also critical as you build your portfolio. Adequate legal protection and insurance coverage is also critical. Always choose people that have real estate investment experience. Assembling a good team requires a lot of vetting to find the best people.

A great real estate agent will do much of that vetting for you and introduce you to the right professionals. Tapping into this valuable network saves you time, money, and stress. A common mistake is working with many agents instead of relying on one. Properly serving an investor takes a great deal of work. Agents are going to bring the best deals first to their most loyal clients.

Find the best agent in the area and establish a solid relationship with him or her. Start the relationship as a two-way street. If the agent doesn't deliver deals, look elsewhere. But overall, it's easier and more profitable to stick with a single agent you trust.

5. Limiting your retirement account to a stock brokerage account

Millions of Americans have retirement accounts consisting of stocks, bonds, and mutual funds. They erroneously think that this money has to stay in an account held at a large financial institution, limited to whatever options offered by that provider. This is false, and those retirement funds can be completely under your control.

It's called a self-directed retirement account, and is exactly what it sounds like: you are in charge of your retirement. You can use that money to invest in real estate if you wish. For many people, the cash flow of real estate has been a far better option than the volatile stock and bond markets. Making the switch to a self-directed IRA isn't hard, and there are many companies that can help with the process.

Tax benefits of real estate

Real estate enjoys a wide array of tax benefits in the U.S. Even as the president and Congress look at budget cuts, many of the major tax benefits of homeownership are likely to survive. However, specific laws and provisions will change from year to year. You should discuss your situation with a knowledgeable tax advisor. This section introduces some of the most important tax benefits. These are quite fundamental and likely to remain in force, but in no way is this section a substitute for a professional.

Tax-free exchanges

When you sell a stock, bond, or other investment that has appreciated, you have to pay capital gains tax unless it's in a retirement account. But what if you could parlay the proceeds of an investment into another investment *without* paying tax, or using a retirement account? Investing in real estate allows you to do just that. This is what savvy real estate investors do to build massive fortunes. Best of all, you can still borrow against the real estate to get cash. You keep the benefits of tax-free appreciation and don't have to keep that money locked away in a retirement account.

These exchanges are commonly referred to as 1031 exchanges, referencing the relevant regulation. They let you parlay one investment into another larger investment as you sell. These 1031 exchanges provide a massive tax benefit, but they must be performed to the letter of the law. There are strict rules and limits, the most important of which is that you have a limited time frame in which to choose the new investment. There are also rules pertaining to the debt carried on the property.

The rules are complex and subject to change. There are entire books written on 1031 exchanges and this is only a brief introduction. What's important for now is to know that this powerful tool exists, and that you can take advantage of it by planning ahead.

Deductions

As an owner of investment property you're entitled to substantial deductions related to your property. You can deduct interest expenses if there's debt on the property. You can also deduct maintenance and improvements.

Many new investors don't know about another major deduction—depreciation. A building's lifespan is only so long before it needs to be rebuilt. The tax code recognizes this and accounts for it as depreciation. You can take a deduction every year you own the building. You can take the deduction even if the property *appreciates* in value. Your tax return shows the benefits of depreciation while your true net worth appreciates!

Leave depreciation to the tax experts, but make sure you ask about it. There are some advanced depreciation strategies you can use when you have a larger real estate portfolio with older buildings. For example, you can accelerate that depreciation by calculating the expected life of your buildings. You'd have to hire an engineer to do these calculations, so it makes sense only for larger properties or portfolios. Even if you're starting small, it's good to know that the tax benefits get better as your portfolio gets bigger.

The basics in this chapter should be sufficient to get you asking the right questions, and avoiding the most common errors. For help finding investments, and people to assist you, please visit **Invest.NoNonsenseBook.com.**

FREQUENTLY ASKED QUESTIONS

Can you represent me on my real estate transaction, or help me find an agent?

I love talking to readers, and will do my best to help. If I cannot help you personally, I can likely direct you to someone who can. Please visit **Help.NoNonsenseBook.Com** for assistance.

What is escrow?

Escrow is a process designed to protect the interests of both buyer and seller, by involving a neutral third party to hold funds and transfer title. The buyer provides the funds to an escrow company. The escrow company verifies that title to the property is clear, and all conditions of the contract have been met. At closing, the escrow company transfers ownership of the property to the buyer, records the documents with the local government, and pays the seller. Please see Chapter 13 for details about the closing process.

What is title insurance? Why do I need it?

Title insurance protects the buyer from losses arising from defects in the title of the property. If someone claims the property, title insurance will pay that claim. You probably won't need it, but you want to have it. You pay the premium once and it is good until ownership changes. Unlike most types of insurance, title insurance protects you against defects in the title that already exist instead of events that occur after you buy the policy.

Do I need to pay for a professional home inspection?

Do you have health insurance, auto insurance, or life insurance? The same prudence applies when thinking about a professional home inspection. A professional inspection protects you from large, unforeseen expenses. It can also put you in a better negotiating position. Ask your agent for a recommendation and carefully vet potential inspectors. Hire someone who makes a thorough inspection and provides a clear and detailed report. Nobody realizes the importance of a meticulous inspection until they find problems after closing. If you cut corners, or just look for the cheapest bid, you do so at your peril.

What does a home warranty cover?

A home warranty protects homeowners against major expenses. These include appliance repairs, air conditioning, heating, electrical, and plumbing. There are differences in coverage between policies, but all have deductibles and limits. There will also be limits on preexisting conditions. The warranty company may ask for the home inspection before it pays a claim. Yet another reason a professional home inspection is invaluable!

Should I overprice my home so I have room to negotiate, or price it at market value?

Overpricing a home deters potential buyers. In general, buyers will not bother with property outside of their range, and you can't always remedy the problem later by reducing the price. Even worse, buyers see homes as "stale" when they've been on market too long; they think there must be something wrong with the house and they don't want to waste their time. For these reasons, it's advisable to price your home close to its expected sales price.

Your real estate agent can calculate a home's optimal asking price based on recent sales and on how sale prices relate to asking prices. For example, if four homes like yours sold for $195,000 and they had an average asking price of $200,000, they sold for 97.5% of the asking price. This shows how much negotiation is common in the current market. In some markets this gap can be large. In others it's negative. Properties in a hot market may sell above listing price with initial offers above asking price. There may even be bidding wars. All real estate is unique and the market evolves. An agent does you no favors by overpricing your house or creating unrealistic expectations.

What is the difference between a real estate agent, a real estate broker, and a realtor?

Most real estate professionals are licensed by the state(s) in which they practice. Licensing ensures they have the education and experience requirements to serve their clients. Consumers usually work with agents. Those agents work under brokers, who process the paperwork, commissions, and handle any disputes. Some brokers work directly with clients as well.

A realtor is a member of the National Association of Realtors, with access to the MLS (Multiple Listing Service) listings in his or her area. Only licensed real estate professionals can become realtors. A real estate agent or broker who is not a realtor will not have access to MLS listings to any greater extent than the general public.

How much should I spend on staging?

Staging is an investment when done right, rather than an expense. Homes that show well sell faster for a higher price. Your home should be as clean and bright as possible. Clutter, dirt, odor, and lack of light can lower the selling price, but they are inexpensive to remedy. Please see Chapter 9 to learn more about staging.

Is a fixed-rate mortgage better than a floating-rate mortgage?

In a perfect world, your rate would be locked for the exact length time you own your home. You wouldn't overpay for locking the interest rate longer than needed, nor would you be at risk for rate fluctuations. But few people can accurately predict how long they will stay in their home. Fixed-rate mortgages give great peace of mind, and how much that is worth to you depends on your overall financial profile and your tolerance of risk. One other consideration is that in most countries, 30 year fixed interest rates are not available. There is even talk about eliminating them in the U.S. For most people, it's sensible to take advantage of the opportunity while it's available.

Should I use the services of a discounted real estate agent?

Buying or selling a home is one of the most important financial decisions most people will ever make. Missed opportunities can have a large impact on your family's lifestyle. Mistakes can be costly. Consequently, it's risky to entrust this important process to a novice because he or she discounts their fees.

As the old proverb says, you get what you pay for. The savings you may see on the top line could turn to a loss through mistakes, missed opportunities, or aggravation. Find an expert, develop a solid relationship, and expect dependable service and valuable expertise. An expert earns you more than your investment in their services.

What's the difference between being pre-qualified and pre-approved for a mortgage?

During the financing process, you will first pre-qualify for a mortgage, then get pre-approved before you have found the specific home you plan to purchase. What is the difference? Pre-qualification is an informal determination by a lender or mortgage broker stating how much you can afford to borrow. Pre-approval is a more thorough qualification, expressing that lender's intent to loan you up to a specified amount. Pre-approval is subject to a final approval based on your financials and the lender's appraisal of the home, but it is generally a reasonable indication of a buyer's ability to close the transaction.

What are closing costs? Who pays them?

Closing costs are fees including escrow and title services, property taxes, real estate agent commissions, homeowners association dues, and loan fees. There is a customary split for common closing costs. These are negotiable but are subject to lender approval. Some loan programs require particular splits for the closing costs. Your escrow officer will be able to explain every line item on the closing statement. For a thorough breakdown of closing costs, see the chart "Closing Costs: Who Pays What" at the end of Chapter 12.

What are contingencies?

Contingencies are escape clauses that allow one of the parties to cancel the transaction without penalty, based on specific conditions. The two most common are a financing contingency and an inspection contingency. The financing contingency makes a sale dependent on the buyers' ability to get a loan. The inspection contingency gives the buyer a chance to cancel the contract after an unsatisfactory inspection. Real estate agents and lawyers may also negotiate other contingencies for special circumstances.

Can I back out of a transaction?

Unless the contract has contingencies that allow you to cancel the contract, there will be consequences to doing so. The consequences will depend on the state and the language of the contract. Buyers typically have more leeway to back out than sellers, most notably during the inspection period.

Sellers who cancel a contract risk a lawsuit from the buyer. The court can force the seller to sell the home and pay damages. Real estate agents also could seek legal recourse if a transaction is cancelled due to a breach of contract. Thus, if you're contemplating backing out of a signed contract to sell your home, talk to a lawyer immediately.

Should I consider buying a foreclosure?

Everyone wants a bargain. If you see a see rock-bottom sale on a recent foreclosure, you may be tempted to buy one yourself. The challenge is that you don't know what you're getting until you buy the property. The protections you enjoy in a traditional sale don't exist. The people that do best with foreclosures buy a lot of them. They have experienced teams and can take a loss. For most people, foreclosures represent far too great a risk.

If prices are out of your budget in your desired area, look for bank foreclosures and short sales. They will give you some of the same protections you'd have in a traditional home sale, at a lower price. Homes that aren't on the market at all may be the best option. Your real estate agent may be able to find one that meets your needs.

What if the home I'm buying doesn't appraise for the purchase price?

It can be unnerving to receive an appraisal that comes in low stating that your dream home isn't worth what you've offered. Before you panic, know that this is common. Appraisals are estimates, and estimates are only as good as the data and the person interpreting them. Banks order appraisals from third-party intermediaries, who assign an appraiser. This system is designed to prevent undue influence on the appraiser, but the appraiser may not be an expert on your particular market.

If you receive a low appraisal, you may be able to cancel the contract depending on the contingencies. However, if you're confident in the value of the home, and you want to proceed, talk to the bank and order another appraisal. You can also contact a different lender, or contemplate seller financing. When an appraisal comes in low, don't panic. Let cooler heads prevail, and the deal will usually get back on track.

How much should I spend on my home? How much should I borrow?

The amount you spend on your home depends on your overall financial picture. Do you expect your income to rise? If so, spending on the higher end of what's affordable makes sense. Or do you think you may need to relocate for work in a few years? A more conservative decision makes sense so that you're not taking as much of a risk, should the market change. The longer you expect to live in your home, and the more stable your financial situation, the more comfortable you can be pushing your budget. If substantial uncertainties are in the cards, buy just enough house to be happy. See Chapter 5 for more information.

When does it *not* make sense to buy a home?

The buy-versus-rent decision varies by region and market cycle. In some places renting is cheaper than buying. In other places the opposite is true. But even if renting is cheaper today, rents are likely to rise with time. Over time, short-term savings can turn into long-run expenditures.

In many areas, there won't be an obvious advantage to buying or renting. The decision will come down to personal preference. The biggest advantage for homeowners is that they can customize their homes to fit their lifestyle. Even if you're allowed to make changes to your rental, you won't want to make major investments. The ability to tailor your living space to your family's lifestyle is a huge benefit.

GLOSSARY

Abstract of title   A summary of the public records relating to the title of a particular piece of land. An attorney or title insurance company reviews an abstract for any title defects that must be cleared before a buyer can consummate the purchase and get title insurance.

Acceleration clause   A condition in a mortgage that may require the balance of the loan to become due immediately if payments are not made or for a breach of other conditions.

Acre   A measure, usually of land, containing 43,560 square feet in any shape.

Ad valorem   Latin phrase that translates to "according to value." A method of taxation using the value of the thing taxed to determine the amount of the tax.

Adverse possession

Colloquially referred to as "squatters' rights," this is a process of acquiring title to real estate by possession for a certain period of time, in addition to other conditions. Conditions vary by state. Adverse possession typically happens on large, remote properties the owners fail to visit or take proper precautions.

Approved attorney

In states where attorneys examine the chain of title before title insurance is issued, the title company will approve certain attorneys as those whose opinion it will accept.

Appurtenance

A right that is a part of the ownership of property, such as a right of way to a highway across the land of another or water rights.

Assumable financing

A note that can be transferred from the existing borrower to a new borrower.

Beneficiary

The person or entity for whose benefit a trust is created. In states in which deeds of trust are commonly used instead of mortgages, the lender (mortgagee) is called the beneficiary.

Binder

A preliminary report as to the condition of a title and a commitment to issue a title insurance policy when certain conditions are met. Sometimes referred to as the "preliminary title report" or "prelim."

Blanket mortgage

A mortgage or trust deed that covers more than one lot or parcel of real property. As individual parcels are sold, there is usually a partial release from the blanket mortgage commensurate with the value of property sold.

Breach of contract

Failure to perform any part of a contract without legal excuse.

Buydown

Payment to the lender resulting in the reduction of the interest rate of a loan. For example, a payment of $10,000 to the lender results in a buydown of the interest rate by 0.5% over the term of the loan.

Carryback

A loan made on a property wherein the seller acts as the lender and thus "carries back" a note at closing.

Clear title

A title to a property that is free and clear of encumbrances. The title company identifies encumbrances on the title report and provides title insurance to protect against any encumbrances that are unknown at closing.

Closing

The date upon which the buyer exchanges funds with the seller for title to the property.

Closing costs

Expenses that buyers and sellers normally incur to complete a transaction in the transfer of ownership. These costs are in addition to the price of the property and are pre-paid at the closing day. Closing costs include escrow fees, title insurance, lender fees, homeowner transfer fees, commissions, and recording fees.

County recorder

A governmental office that maintains public records and documents that disclose the owner of a property and any recorded liens on the property.

Deed

A document that transfers title to real property from one owner to another. The deed should contain an accurate description of the property being conveyed, should be signed and witnessed according to the laws of the state where the property is located. It should be delivered to the purchaser at closing.

Deed of trust

Like a mortgage, an instrument whereby real property is given as security for a debt. However, in a deed of trust there are three parties to the instrument: the borrower, the trustee and the lender (or beneficiary). The borrower transfers the legal title for the property to the trustee, who holds the property in trust as security for the payment of the debt to the lender or beneficiary. If the borrower pays the debt as agreed, the deed of trust becomes void. If, however, the borrower defaults in the payment of the debt, the trustee may sell the property at a public sale, under the terms of the deed of trust. In most jurisdictions where the deed of trust is in force, the borrower is subject to having his/her property sold without benefit of legal proceedings. Foreclosures involving deeds of trust are referred to as non-judicial foreclosures.

Deed restrictions   Limitations in the deed to a property that dictate certain uses that may or not be made of the property. Deed restrictions affect the value of property if the restrictions limit valuable uses.

Down payment   The initial upfront portion of the total cost that serves as collateral to show the buyer is a suitable candidate. The down payment is commonly 20% of the total cost of the property. The parties may agree on a different amount.

Due diligence   The buyer's inspection and investigation before buying a property.

Due-on-sale clause   A clause in a promissory note requiring that the full balance of a loan is due upon the sale or the transfer of title to a property. Lenders rarely enforce this clause, but they have the right to do so.

Earnest deposit   Money the buyer deposits to escrow to show good faith. The money is refundable upon certain contingencies such as inspection and financing.

Easement   A right-of-way granted to a person or company allowing access to or over the owner's land. An electric company may have a right-of-way across private property.

Equitable title   The ability to use and enjoy a property. This is distinct from legal title. One can have equitable title but not legal title.

Encroachment   An obstruction or building that intrudes beyond a legal boundary onto neighboring land.

Encumbrance   A legal right or interest in land that affects a good or clear title and diminishes the land's value. It can take numerous forms such as zoning ordinances, easements, mortgages, liens, pending legal action, unpaid taxes, or restrictive covenants. An encumbrance does not legally prevent transfer of the property to another. A title search should reveal encumbrances. It is up to the buyer whether to buy with the encumbrance or try to remove it.

Endorsement

Addition to or modification of a title insurance policy that changes coverage of the policy, fulfilling the insured's requirements.

Escheat

The reversion of property to the state when an owner dies without heirs or claimants.

Escrow

A process involving a neutral third party that holds money and items of value for the buyer and seller and conducts the transaction for both parties' protection.

Eviction

The legal process for removal of a tenant in violation of a lease agreement.

Fee simple

An estate under which the owner is entitled to unrestricted powers to dispose of the property, and which can be left by will or inherited.

Fixtures — Personal property that is attached to real property and is legally treated as real property while attached. Examples are chandeliers, medicine cabinets, and window blinds.

Foreclosure — The situation in which the lender takes over title to a property because a homeowner failed to make mortgage payments. Depending on the state, this process may happen privately through a pre-appointed trustee or through the court system in front of a judge.

General warranty deed — A deed that conveys all the grantor's interests in, and title to, the property to the grantee, and warrants that if the title is defective or has a "cloud" on it (such as mortgage claims, tax liens, or judgments), the grantee may hold the grantor liable.

Grant — To transfer an interest in real property, either the fee simple or a lesser interest, such as an easement.

Grantee — The party in the deed who is the buyer or recipient.

Grantor — The party in the deed who is the seller or giver.

Hard money lender   A private lender, who typically lends at rates substantially higher than a bank but with more flexible criteria. See Private Money Loans

Hazard insurance   Insurance to cover the cost of property damage caused by fire, storms, and other common hazards.

Impounds   Accounts established by lenders for the accumulation of borrowers' funds to make future payments of taxes, mortgage insurance premiums, and insurance premiums.

Joint tenancy   An undivided interest in property taken by two or more people. The interests must be equal and start at the same time. When a joint tenant died the interest passes to the surviving joint tenants.

Judgment lien   An involuntary lien against the property of a judgment debtor.

Land contract   An installment contract for the sale of land whereby the seller holds legal title and the buyer has equitable title until the buyer pays the full sale price. Also referred to as Contract for Deed or Installment Sale.

Lease purchase
A transaction in which the tenant can buy the home during or at the end of her lease. The parties establish the price in advance and the buyer may use a portion of the monthly rent towards the down payment.

Legal description
A description of land recognized by law, based on government surveys, spelling out property's exact boundaries.

Lender's policy
A title insurance policy that insures the validity, enforceability, and priority of a lender's lien.

Lien
An encumbrance on a property such as a promissory note, property tax lien, or mechanic's lien.

Mechanic's lien
A lien created by statute to secure priority of payment for work performed and materials furnished in construction or repair of property.

Mortgage banker
A specialized lending institution that lends money solely with respect to real estate and secures its loans with mortgages or deeds of trust.

Mortgage broker
A person or company that arranges loans for another on commission.

Mortgage insurance	Insurance written by a mortgage insurance company protecting the lender against loss incurred by a default.
Negative amortization	A loan whose principal balance increases after the borrower makes a payment because the required payment is less than the accumulated interest.
Note	See Promissory Note
Option	An agreement offering the right to purchase a property for a particular amount of money within a specified period of time.
Owner's policy	A policy of title insurance usually insuring an owner of real estate against loss occasioned by defects in, liens against, or unmarketability of the owner's title. This is distinct from the Lender's Policy.
PITI	Abbreviation for principal, interest, taxes and insurance, all of which some lenders may lump together in one monthly payment.
PMI	Abbreviation for private mortgage insurance. An insurance contract that protects the lender in the event that the borrower defaults on the loan. Lenders

	will require PMI when a buyer makes a low down payment on a loan.
Points	A one-time fee the borrower pays up-front to the lender, sometimes in exchange for a slightly lower mortgage rate. One point equals one percent of the total amount of the loan.
Pre-payment	Payment of a mortgage loan, or part of it, before the due date. Loan agreements sometimes restrict the right of pre-payment by limiting the amount that can be pre-paid in any one year or charging a penalty for pre-payment.
Private money loan	A loan made by a private party (instead of a bank) that typically consist of large down payments, high interest rates, and short terms.
Promissory note	A signed document that is a promise to pay a certain amount of money by a particular time, along with specified interest payments.
Quitclaim deed	A deed that transfers whatever interest the maker of the deed may have in the particular parcel of land. A quitclaim deed is often given to clear the title when the grantor's interest in a property is questionable. By accepting

such a deed the buyer assumes all the risks. Such a deed makes no warranties as to the title. It simply transfers to the buyer whatever interest the grantor has.

Reconveyance

A document used to transfer title from a trustee to the equitable owner of real estate, when title is held as collateral for a debt. This is most commonly used upon payment in full of a trust deed. Also called a deed of reconveyance or release.

Recording

Filing documents affecting real estate as a matter of public record, giving notice to future purchasers, creditors or other interested parties. Recording is controlled by statutes that vary by region, and usually requires witnessing and notarizing to be recorded.

Re-finance

The action of obtaining a new loan in order to pay off an existing loan.

Rent to own

see Lease Purchase

Riparian rights

The rights of owners of property bordering bodies of water relating to the water and its use.

Seller financing

Financing for the purchase of a home whereby the seller acts as the lender.

Setback   Required distances for the location of structures in relation to the perimeter of the property. Setbacks are controlled by local zoning ordinance. Homeowners' associations may add other restrictions.

Short sale   A real estate transaction where the seller's lender accepts to sell the home for less than the current balance due on the loan.

Special assessments   A tax imposed on property, individual lots, or all property in the immediate area, for road construction, sidewalks, sewers, streetlights, etc.

Surface rights   Rights to enter upon and use the surface of a parcel of land, usually in connection with an oil and gas lease, or other mineral lease.

Survey   A map or plate a licensed surveyor makes that shows the results of measuring the land with its elevations, improvements, boundaries, and relationship to surrounding properties.

Tax sale   A public sale of property at auction by a governmental authority after a period of non-payment of property tax. The tax sale process is controlled by local statute and differs between regions.

Tenancy by the entirety Ownership by married persons where each owns the entire estate, with the survivor taking the whole upon the other's death.

Tenancy in common An estate or interest in land held by two or more persons, each having equal rights of possession, but without any right of succession by survivorship between the owners.

Title company Provides insurance against claims on title so buyer and seller are protected after close of escrow.

Title defect Any claim, right, or irregularity in a chain of title that is adverse to the claim of ownership.

Title officer An officer who searches for title claims that could put the buyer's right to a property at risk.

Trustee sale A public auction of the title to a property after a borrower defaults on a loan.

Turnkey A home needing no repairs or modifications. The buyer can "turn the key" and move in.

Unlisted homes   A home where the current owners have not publicly displayed an interest to sell, not listing on MLS or other public sources.

VA guarantee   An insurance contract in which the Veterans Administration (VA) protects the lender against a default by the borrower.

Warranty deed   A deed used in many states to convey title to real estate. A warranty deed contains provisions under which the seller becomes liable to the purchaser for defects in the title.

Zoning   Laws passed by local governments regulating the size, type, structure, nature, and use of land or buildings.

ABOUT THE AUTHOR

A lex Goldstein has acted as principal in over $50 million of real estate transactions, from homes to office buildings and large parcels of land. He currently represents clients on residential and commercial transactions.

Alex has authored several books, is an honors graduate of Northwestern University, and was also a visiting scholar at Oxford University.

Food and wine are his life-long passions, he has served on the boards of the International Wine & Food Society and La Confrérie des Chevaliers du Tastevin. Alex resides in Scottsdale, Arizona.

BONUS FOR READERS

Thank you for reading this book. My goal was to produce a simple, no nonsense approach that was practical and actionable without overwhelming you.

Now, if you're wondering what your next steps are or you'd like some additional help, here's what to do now:

Visit **Bonus.NoNonsenseBook.com**

This is where you will find the bonus resources and material we've produced for you.

Video Presentation

The author's presentation of the concepts in this book, and answers to readers' questions, is available to all readers at no cost. Please visit **Bonus.NoNonsenseBook.com** to view the presentation.

Help Finding an Agent or Being Represented by the Author

The author represents people in luxury and investment transactions. If you're looking for these types of properties in the area we serve, we may be able to help you directly.

Most readers will be in other states, but we can still help. We have a network of agents and investors around the country, and would be happy to make introductions. If we don't have a resource in your area, we may be able to help you vet one.

Please visit **Help.NoNonsenseBook.com** to tell us more about your needs.

Investing in Real Estate

From evaluating investment properties to how to setup a self-directed IRA, help is available at **Invest.NoNonsenseBook. com**

Made in the USA
Monee, IL
28 October 2022

16754711R00094